Sixty Gold Pieces

Writings by Thirty-Six Authors

Editorial Committee

Sharon Alvarado   Larry Mason   Robert Reid
Doris Thome   Beth Thompson

Cover Art

Paul Edwards

Proof Reader

Christine Riesenfeld

Published by Sixty Gold Pieces

ISBN 978-1-257-93957-2

Distribution: Bookstores can purchase *Sixty Gold Pieces* directly from the authors. Order online (www.lulu.com). All proceeds, above the cost of publishing this book, will be donated to the Santa Barbara City College Foundation.

Dedication

To

Joan Fallert

The tireless teacher
Who guides our growth

And

In Memory of

Bill Downey

Who Planted the Seeds

Foreword

In *Recollections and Writing,* an adult education class in Santa Barbara, twenty to forty writers come together weekly to share our tales.

Prose or poems, we listen to our instructor read each piece. We hear what we did not see in our own story; repetition, uncomfortable wordage, the use of to be, all "hang-nails" come to light.

Dead silence after a reading usually indicates the piece needs work. Ideally we hear comments. The teacher points out a detail, a class member questions a word or line, another suggests the story end sooner and our work gets better.

All of these pieces have been read in class and they reflect the rich life experiences of their contributors.

Sixty Gold Pieces
Contents

Making a Poem out of Nothing

By Joan Fallert

Whatever I am thinking has stopped short

of recollection   a short phrase no longer there

no longer shifting   skirting consciousness

skidding around   in the back of my mind like-

like what   Since I can't remember I can't say

what it is like   now that it is not

Nothing triggers the remembering

no smell   no sound   no touch   no image startles

even one word to cluster around about into thought

-and suddenly poppies-couldn't be farther afield

not a thing to do with anything that came before-

just a common California wildflower I saw

blooming like hell all over the foothills   capering

between the guard rails on the highway   patches of

saucy color circling the serpentine rock   tucked under

fallen oak branches   carpeting the meadow-

What other way can you say it – poppies laid right

to the edge of the next rise like a great rug tacked

tight against the horizon   and in the breeze

I can see them ripple the slopes of the mountain

I cannot forget – yellow-tipped impudent orange-

orange explodes unabashed in my head

Worlds Meet

"Walk long enough and we all trade places."

Flight 167 to Tel Aviv

By Robert Reid

El Al flight 167 to Tel Aviv stood on the tarmac at La Guardia ready to be cleared for takeoff. Mrs. Schwartz was seated in First Class, seat 1C and her beloved Scottish Terrier, Tevye, for which she had purchased a first class seat was in his pet carrier in 1D. A very large man in a dark suit approached her from the Coach section. She noticed that a curly black wire emanated from the collar of his suit coat and ended in an ear plug on the right. Must be security, she thought. El Al has the best security.

"Mrs. Schwartz?" the burly man asked.

"Yes, I'm Mrs. Schwartz. What is it?"

Her inquisitor flashed an identification card and responded, "I'm agent Kupperman of the Mossad and we have been assisting the Prime Minister during negotiating sessions here in New York and he is traveling incognito back to Israel on this flight. We note that your dog has the only open First Class seat and wonder if we might make other arrangements for him and accommodate the Prime Minister.

"Well, I don't know if I want to do that to Tevye.

"We can put Tevye in the rear galley" the agent interrupted. He will be out of passengers' way and will do fine back there."

Mrs. Schwartz pondered the situation for a while. The dog probably would be fine in the back. She was loyal to her embattled Israel and had enormous respect for the Prime Minister. Besides having him to herself for the 10 hour flight was irresistible.

"All right." she said. "But be careful with Tevye, he's very important to me."

After two Mossad agents got the Prime Minister settled in seat 1D, the plane was cleared for take-off. Mrs. Schwartz had a lovely time discussing politics and world events with the leader of her country who politely parried her questions and accepted her advice of which there was plenty. The head of state who was accustomed to snoozing on these flights found there was no rest on this trip.

The plane was starting its final approach for Tel Aviv. The Mossad agent decided to check on the dog so as to bring it forward immediately upon landing. He opened the door to the pet carrier and was shocked to find that the dog was dead.

"My God!" he said to his fellow agent. "What are we going to do?" We promised Mrs. Schwartz we would take good care of the dog. What will the Prime Minister think?"

His partner thought for a moment and said, "I think we can make this work. Here is my plan."

The plane landed and began to taxi to the gate. The second Mossad agent came to seat IC. "Mrs. Schwartz, I don't know if you realize this but pets brought into Israel have to be quarantined for 3 weeks before they can be released."

"No, I didn't know. What shall I do?"

"Well, you've been so accommodating about the seat for the Prime Minister we will put you up at the Tel Aviv Hilton for the 3 weeks, totally at state expense, and bring the dog to you when it is out of quarantine."

Mrs. Schwartz thought for a moment. She really didn't have anything urgent to do and 3 weeks at the luxurious Hilton would be a treat.
"Okay, I accept your offer and thanks."

After the unfortunate dog owner was limousined to the Hilton and properly ensconced in the Presidential Suite, the Mossad went to work. An agent flew to Scotland and obtained a Terrier with identical conformation to Mrs. Schwarz's dog. They trained it to respond to the name Tevye; schooled him in the usual tricks. They even broke into Mrs. Schwarz's hotel room and stole a garment so the dog could get to recognize the scent of his new owner. All the while Mrs. Schwartz was taking full advantage of the government's largess by ordering room service, using the spa each day and consuming large amounts of Dom Perignon champagne.

Finally the 3 weeks were over and there was a knock on the door of the Presidential Suite. Mrs. Schwartz opened the door to the Mossad agent who held a Scottish Terrier in his arms. He stepped in, set the dog on the floor and the little pup scampered around the room a bit before stopping in front of Mrs. Schwartz. He looked up at her and wagged his tail vigorously. The agent was jubilant. The dog recognized its master. All that work had paid off. No agency was better at escaping from a tight situation than the Mossad.

His reverie was shattered when Mrs. Schwartz said, "That's not my dog."

"What do you mean that's not your dog? Look how he comes to you! You're his mistress!"

"I tell you, that is not my dog."

"Why isn't that your dog? It's a Scottish Terrier, answers to the name Tevye and recognizes you as his mistress."

"That is not my dog!"

"Well tell me why you believe that is not your dog."

"My dog was dead. I was bringing him back to Israel for burial."

England. June 6th 1944

By Audrey E. Martinson

The scent of roses heavy in the air, grass dewy under my feet. Sweet sunshine filters through the leaves of the old mulberry tree, my favorite place of refuge. Such an anomaly to be in this lovely peaceful setting and hear, in the background, the mutter of heavy guns, the sharper rat-tat-tat of anti-aircraft fire.

Fearful, my senses are alert, my heart and mind fly over that narrow strip of water known as the English Channel. Waldo, my fiancé, left two days ago. After six months of preparation he did not tell me where or when, just: "This is it!"

I watched him bicycle away from the house and thought of the many false alarms we had lived through in the past months. One time they – the 47th regiment of the 9th Infantry Division – were gone for a whole week. When they came back Waldo was exhausted, wan and very thoughtful. "Where were you?" I said.

"Just an exercise."

Only twenty-three years old, but he was already a hardened veteran of North Africa and Sicily. At twenty I have become so used to a state of war. I can hardly remember a time when nights were undisturbed by sirens and bomb blasts. Nor a time when food, heating fuel and clothes were plentiful.

And now this is the day we had been waiting for. Dreading this parting, knowing it has to be to get this war over with.

The gunfire is heavier. I can feel the vibrations of the ground, and the air, too, is roused from its sleepy summer torpor by the distant roar of a multitude of planes. Are they ours? I can only hope and pray that they are. And this beautiful weather, so different from the storms we have been having, will this help the boy-men who are risking their lives to save this out-of-kilter world?

Questions. No answers yet

Her eyes. Her eyes spoke to me without words, hand gentle on my arm.

This was the beginning of many visits. The shades always pulled. No family, no visitors, no telephone, the house heavy with grief.

Mr. Goldman never spoke to me. He would come into the kitchen, look at me, nod his head and disappear into a back room.

Mrs. Goldman would sit, look at me and pat my hand. Sometimes we would talk. She would tell me to "be patient." Often we could hear my stepmother, her anger hot and violent. We would be silent together.
She never hurried me.
We would sit until I found the courage to go home.

One day I returned from school.
The shades were up.
The house was empty.
There were no Jews living next door.
My friend was gone.

The Day My Pastor Got In Trouble

By Doris Wells Miller

In 1943 World War II was in full swing. Dearborn, Michigan, my hometown, was a naval base and the heart of the war effort. The Ford Motor Company and General Motors were deeply involved in turning out tanks and airplane parts. Patriotic feelings were very strong.

My father was an air raid warden. His job was to patrol the neighborhood every evening to make sure everyone's curtains were drawn so no light could shine out and give the enemy a target. He built wooden shutters for the windows in the basement where we were to go when we heard the sirens warning of enemy planes overhead.

The Methodist church I attended had a great youth program. I was about 12 year's old, attended Sunday school, active in the youth group and sang in the choir. Our pastor was a good and caring man. My first camping experience was at a camp about 150 miles north. During the church service I actually listened to his sermons. I had heard that he was a "pacifist" which I (kind of) understood that he believed in peace.

It was Halloween and both young and old were invited to a party at the parsonage. We were to come in costume. The youth party was in the basement and the adults were upstairs. We played some games and had some food. During the games a policeman came halfway down the basement stairs. The leader asked if there was a problem.

The policeman said, "That's okay; go on with your games."

When he left, the pastor and his wife came downstairs and said, "There is something we must tell you."

Pastor Geer walked over to a door at the back of the room, opened it and half a dozen oriental people came out. They were petite, very polite and bowed and said "tank you" in their broken English.

The pastor then asked us to take off our costumes and give them to the "little people" he called "Nisei." We did as we were asked and the "little people" put them on and he led them out of the house. An adult told us that the party was over and if anyone needed a ride they would drive us home.

I did not understand what had happened until a friend from the church came to my home and explained how our pastor had been spiriting American-born Japanese out of the camps in the West and hiding them in his basement. He was part of the Underground Railroad that moved them into Canada. He was using the church camp in central Michigan as a half-way house for the Nisei.

Evidently, the police had found out about his illegal activities and were waiting outside for us to leave the party so they could raid the house. Of course, the children that had already left were the Nisei in our costumes. I never saw my favorite pastor again and I have always wondered what happened to him until moving to Vista del Monte. It was on our first night at dinner when Bob Ogilvie found out where I had lived and asked a few questions. He told me his wife was the sister of Mrs. Geer, the pastor's wife. He assured me that everyone safely escaped. The Geers had retired to San Diego where they had passed away about ten years ago.

Catwalk

By Christine Riesenfeld

Dressed **in black tights** and turtleneck, I was curled up with Stefan on our couch on the top floor of our Physic Place flat watching some BBC program on the telly. The July night was warm and moonlit, so we opened the balcony door and our cat, "Beau" made a beeline for the terrace. He had taken to jumping up on the thin terrace railing that seemed incapable of supporting his ample feline body.

Out of the corner of my eye, I saw something leap from the terrace railing up towards our roof. We both head a "PLOP!" and ran on to the terrace. No Beau. I turned and looked up at the steeply-pitched slate roof and there he was; looking proud but not quite sure of his footing. Many years earlier, Beau's Pennsylvania veterinarian had told us he was a bit cross-eyed; a weakness that would not serve him well trying to negotiate steep London roofs.

After much cajoling, it was clear that Beau was afraid to come back down the roof to our terrace. Never fear! I would crawl up to the rescue. Why hadn't Stefan offered? Oh, that's right; someone had to hold the flashlight. Just as I had scrambled halfway up the steep slates, Beau disappeared to the other side of the roof. Feeling like Cary Grant in "To Catch a Thief," I lowered my self onto the terrace and we ran down the stairs and out to the front door to see if we could spot him from there.

Unfortunately, our London flat was a mews house, similar in composition to the attached townhouses in the U.S. This opened all sorts of new horizons for our Beau. We thought we caught sight of him disappearing into our neighbors' open terrace door. Now what? At 10 p.m. our neighbors and best friends, Charae and Henrik Sorensen, were probably in bed, but we had no choice. It would be better to warn them than to have them awakened by a cat fight between their cat, Bluey, and our happy wanderer.

An aside on the Sorensens: Charae was born in Baton Rouge, Louisiana and had lived in Paris, Riyadh and now London. Her Danish husband, Henrik, was the administrative consul for the Danish Embassy. That meant he had to "handle" everything for the ambassador. He is the super-organized, can-do Dane. Charae strolls through life at Bayou speed, thoroughly enjoying every slow minute of it. Their relationship epitomizes the phrase, "opposites attract."

Back to Beau. Charae answered the phone, giggling and said, "I think Beau just passed through the bedroom, but he's gone back out the balcony door. Do you want me to help look?"

At this point Stefan waved to me from outside our front door and I said, "Just keep Beau there if he shows up again."

When I went outside, Stefan said, "Bad news. I think he just entered the flat on the other side of the Sorensens."

Unfortunately, this was our new neighbor, Alice, who had moved in less than a month ago and we'd never met. Stefan said, "Maybe we should let Beau spend the night there. We'll call her in the morning."

I doubted she or Beau would agree with Stefan's suggestion, so I walked to the front of her house. The lights were still on inside. I knocked quietly on her door, secretly hoping she'd gone to bed. She hadn't. Alice opened the door and welcomed me in to look around.

As I climbed the narrow spiral staircase, Alice said, "He might be in Great-aunt Ann's room, she's 85 and probably asleep. As soon as we walked in we saw Beau curled up on Great-aunt Ann's bed. He bolted off the bed and ran out the terrace door.

Great-aunt Ann sat up in bed saying, "What's going on?"

Before I could gather my courage to respond, Alice said, "No bother, Auntie, it was just a cat."

Great-aunt Ann looked relieved and laid back down. I apologized and ran back out into the mews.

Now what? Stefan ran into our house to answer the phone; it was Charae calling. Beau was back in their house and she closed the terrace door so he could not escape. She said, "Tell Christine to come on over and get him."

I raced up the stairs as quietly as possible in case their daughter, Christina, was asleep. Charae motioned me into their bedroom. She was no longer giggling; she was convulsing with laughter. I asked, "What's so funny? Where's Henrik?"

She said, "You, you look like a cat burglar all dressed in black. Henrik is naked and hiding in the bathroom!" By this point she was practically on the floor, laughing uncontrollably.

I looked around and saw a tail sticking out from under their bed. Before it disappeared, I reached under and scoped Beau out. With Beau's claws sunken into my turtleneck and all the mews houses alight by now. I carried him back to our house. From that day forward "mews" houses had a new meaning for us.

Two Views – One Goodbye

By Doris Thome

A **hospital bed** next to a window in Abbey's living room is now where she spends her time. She's watched skies change, flowers fade, and leaves fall. Three colorful leaves have hung tenaciously onto the magnificent liquidamber. Until last night when unseen by human eyes, two of the leaves silently broke free, and parasailed to the ground. One lone crimson leaf remains.

> *You hang on like it's going to make a difference. Come on, come on. You've won. You're the champion. We made a deal and you can't cheat. I've got to be awake to see you go. No bailing out in the middle of the night, like these last two guys. We have an agreement. When you leave, I leave. That's the deal.*

Scooter has barely left Abbey's side. He eats two squares a day, takes potty breaks, and ventures out to chase the birds as a substitute for their beach runs. Scooter rests on a pillow next to

Abbey's shoulder. It's uncomfortable for Abbey
to have even her beloved dog plop down too
close. Abbey hasn't eaten in, what is it now,
fifteen—sixteen days? She says her body can no
longer handle food. It's readying itself. Abbey
was given a prognosis of three months. That was
two months ago.

*Here I am with a get-out-of-town pass. At first I
thought, no way. Soon I realized it is what it is.
Now, all I do is wait. No one wants to hear this.
My reality raises their defenses. They judge my
opinions as depression. I shouldn't think like this,
they utter. Excuse me, since when has fact
become depression. You would think dying was a
four-letter word. Everything dies. My friends are
part of this adventure and what is truly
important is what each of us feels. Sharing this
would be the ultimate gift.*
*Lone leaf...you're still here, red against the blue
sky. Is your color fading? Are your edges curling
a might? Well, my coloring isn't all that great
either. Perhaps it's time to renege on the
agreement we made. Maybe I won't wait for you.
It's time... Please...Let go.*

And it does. Abbey's pain wanes. In slow motion the solo leaf moves horizontal, like a kite catching an updraft. Abbey moves her hand closer to her beloved Scooter. The leaf spirals and Abbey whispers, "Yes!"

Scooter lifts his head. Nose raised and eyes closed he gives a long mournful howl, and...snuggles his head into Abbey's...lifeless palm.

Algiers

By Paul Barrett

Ah! That night in Algiers
She said, "Let's leave the party"
We rode our horses out into the desert
There was a full moon

Indian Omelet

By Sandra Williams

Yippee! For the past 30 days lunches and dinners had featured smooth, rich, ice cream. The perfect diet. The free-range cows which produced the best ice cream I've ever tasted ate whatever they wanted. Popular flavors included mango, coconut, cashew, pistachio and vanilla.

Awestruck, I observed every person, animal, flower, brilliant color and sweet smell of India as I hung my head out the bus window through most of northern and southern India in the spring of 1997. By western standards, the people in India had nothing. They lived in mud or cow dung huts with dirt floors, no running water, and no electricity. They washed their gorgeous, colorful silk saris in streams or a bucket from the local well and draped them over bushes to dry.

Their huge smiles flashed perfect, brilliant white teeth against warm brown skin. Their black eyes danced. Their enormous hearts radiated inner peace, a childlike innocence and bliss. They were curious, gentle spirits. What was their secret? Having nothing...was that a clue?

From what I experienced, no one in India worried about house payments, having a new Lexus, finding Mr. Right, getting twenty million dollars in the bank, being president of the company, having a perfect figure or traveling around the world. Such are transient things which can go as easily as they come and don't necessarily bring lasting happiness.

I spent the last night of my trip in Varanasi. Before dawn, I embarked on a small boat down the Ganges River which flows from the Himalayas to the Indian Ocean. As the sun rose, I floated a candle on the sacred water to release my prayers to the universe. The shore was lined with sandalwood funeral pyres sending flames to heaven next to people bathing, cleansing their souls on the steps leading into the river. Varanasi is known as the holiest city in the world.

I returned to the hotel and packed for my flight. Tomorrow I had to be in Delhi to catch my flight to Hong Kong. After a month of love, peace, silence and meditation, I had five days to reacclimate before returning to my real life in Santa Barbara.

I found out that a pilot strike had grounded all flights. With no reservations and crossed fingers, I rushed to the train station. The only available seat was unreserved in second class. I stood for three hours waiting for the train; the crowd shoved me, along with my two suitcases, into the closest car as the train was still rolling to a stop. I grabbed a solo bench seat along the side rather than going to the open compartment that seated six people. Sweat dripped off the tip of my nose as I sat down. A sea of curious faces stared at me from the open compartments in our car.

I burst into tears as heat, exhaustion and the relief of finally having a seat overpowered me. People stared with concern...why was this crazy six foot-tall American woman crying? I spoke no Hindi and I felt like a prisoner with no control or concept of what lay ahead.

The same huge red sun I watched rise that morning as I floated on the Ganges River now slipped below the horizon, stealing the landscape with it. Dim train lights went on; Indian passengers still stared at me; I must be better than television. I remember my husband scolding me in line at the market for staring. I replied, "I'm just watching." Is that what these people were doing?

How was I going to sleep? What if I was robbed or attacked during the night? What would I use for a pillow?

A jillion hours passed. The interior lights dimmed. I used my purse as a pillow on the hard wooden bench. I flipped on my side, bending my long legs as I swung them up. It was hard to fit six feet on a short Indian train bench. My blanket covered me from shoulder to knees. In the fetal position, I attempted sleep while the intrigued audience gazed at my size eleven feet.

At dawn, a scrubby Indian boy walked through the car hawking dirty omelets. I hadn't eaten since breakfast yesterday. I was famished. Somehow I knew the omelet served with toast and *chai* would be safe for me to eat.

Where did the boy cook, since the train had not stopped? Did he have a campfire between the cars? Finally my made-to-order breakfast arrived. I carefully cut a small bit of omelet. The soot from the campfire added an intriguing smoky taste. I enjoyed the fluffiness of the eggs, which were light and melted in my mouth. I chewed each bit until it dissolved before I swallowed. Still the gang watched.

The thick slice of toast had grill marks across it. I surmised that butter would take away from the crunchy, nutty flavor. Again, I took small bites to have it last longer. The *chai* was truly the sweet nectar of the gods—warm, sweet, creamy and a tonic to my body and soul.

I looked up to see my new friends enjoying my experience as much as I. This delicious humble meal sensuously consumed by me was a sign of my acceptance of the people, their culture and their food. It was obvious they were glad that I was feeling better. They had succeeded in watching over and protecting me.

At last, the train pulled into the Delhi station in time for me to get to the airport for my international flight. As a final gift, my train mates stood aside as I rose to leave, creating a path for my departure off the train. Their never-ending grins filled their faces as they waved farewell. Happy tears rolled down my cheeks as I waved and smiled. The concern, honor, respect, and energy shared over the last 18 hours with this humble group of genuine people was typical of my visit in India.

When I arrived at the Peninsula Hotel in Hong Kong, I realized the clothes and jewelry—the "stuff" I thought important—was just taking up space in my mind and closet. I gave my Room Butler nearly all of the $7,000 worth of clothes I had bought at Saks 5th Avenue in Beverly Hills before my trip. It was much easier traveling home with minimal baggage.

Back in Santa Barbara, I drop off bags of clothing at the local rescue mission and donate other items at the thrift store. I own one set of sheets, one set of towels and one dressy outfit (the same Ellen Tracy blazer I wore throughout India). I wear everyday clothes, no jewelry, no makeup and a wash-and-wear hairstyle. It is a constant joy to purge the physical and mental "stuff" to make room for inner peace.

My days are now simple. I enjoy the beauty of nature, see the good in people and life, dedicate my life to service, especially animals. I share what I have. There is always enough. I meditate daily and teach meditation through the Deepak Chopra Center. I associate with positive, loving, giving people and I avoid negativity. I also avoid violence in person, in the newspaper and in my thoughts. I seldom listen to the radio. In enjoy the silence of the present moment in which I live and feel a freedom that is filled with love and forgiveness.

Enamored

"One of the sweetest joys in life is to have someone read to you"

My First Love

By Allen Zimmer

The day I saw her coming up the block, it was love at first sight. Her soft flowing curves, her perfect proportions, she gave off a sense of power, but in a refined way. She was my first and when I finally got into her I was immediately and forever transformed from an awkward boy into full manhood.

She was a beauty, a '39 Ford 2 door coupe.

She was completely shaved, and had two skirts. Her seven coats of black hand-polished lacquer shone brightly wherever we went. Every time I looked at her I'd see myself reflected perfectly in her mirrored finish. I'd take out my comb, check my flattop, my wings and ducks ass. Like the words to that song, "Life's just a dream, Shaboom."

At least it was until the night she had her major breakdown, and her "sha" went "ka-boom." After that we didn't go out, just stayed home night after night. A guy in the '50s in the San Fernando Valley without wheels was a nobody, a nothing.

Then my uncle called and said he had a surprise for me. The next day he towed us back to his place and said "stay there, I'll be back." After what seemed like forever, he pulled up with a big smile on his face and in the back of his truck was an engine block. It kinda looked stock, but bigger, much bigger.

Then some of his friends came by and tools appeared from everywhere, along with a large cooler of beer. They quickly removed the spent engine and then hoisted the new large block into place, gently sliding it down between her smooth round fenders, stopping only when they heard her groan as she gave way under the weight.

When they were finished, they replaced her hood, restoring her dignity and beauty. My uncle nodded at me, "Go ahead, fire her up."

I gently slipped in my key, gave it a turn, and pushed her round starter button. She trembled a little, but then began purring like a kitten.

They all hoisted their bottles in salute, and with contented smiles they lighted up, taking deep drags, sending smoke rings curling in the air above her. My uncle saw my eager look and grinned, "Show us what she'll do."

So I dropped it into first, pushed hard to the floor, she let out a delightful squeal as we took off. I threw it up firmly into second. She obediently squealed again.　When I sensed she was about to explode, I drove it down into third.　Another squeal.

Bitch'n.　Rubber in third gear.　I'm back.

The Cat With the Great Green Eyes and the Dog With the Wigwag Tail.

A Purrfect Bedtime Story.

By Marilou Shiells

Here is the story
of the deeds and the glory
of the cat with the great green eyes
and the dog with the wigwag tail.

There once was a curious kitten,
about whom much should be written.
Her eyes were a green, that is seldom seen;
except in the crown of a Queen.

At the same time there arrived
in a litter of five
a pup with a wigwag tail.
He seemed at a glance
to be doing a dance
he was so happy to be alive.

When that sweet little kitten
was young she was smitten
with the pup with a wig wag tail.

And that love was steadfast
and would last and last
despite problems that that would entail.

As they grew older
and ever more bolder
they set out on adventures galore.
Unlike the gingham dog and the calico cat
who had that horrible vicious spat
they remained friends for ever more

There was that time
they tracked down a mime
intending to have a chat.
Little did they surmise
(it came as quite a surprise)
that the mime was as mute as a bat.

The cat with the great green eyes
and the dog with the wigwag tail
once did depart
for the Museum of Art
to look at a painting for sale.
But they fell in love
not with the above

but with a sculpture of the tail of a whale.

One time they were wishing
that they could go fishing
off of a very long pier.
But decided instead
to go back to bed
and dream of that pier so dear.

One Sunday they encountered a mouse
and chased it all over the house.
They were ready to drop
when the mouse begged them to stop
as it was time to be nice
to all mice.

Off went the pair
Mostly on a dare
In an old leaky boat
sometimes sailing, lots of time bailing
Just keeping that old boat afloat

As the duo cruised the ocean
they were quite upset by the motion
the ups and the downs and

the downs and the ups
quickly discouraged the notion

One hot day they went to the Zoo
hoping for a glimpse of a gnu
once they were there
they spied a polar bear
and sat on the ice so-o-o-o nice

Then on a lark
They went to the park
to go riding the carousel
the cat caught the ring and began to sing
and the dog let out a huge bark

Once when the circus came to town
the dog wished he could be a clown
but then they thought "to be famous
they would have to tame us"
and the wish was soon voted down.

Thus ends this story
of the deeds and the glory
of the cat with the great green eyesand the dog with
the wigwag tail.

Memories of the 'Mallard'

By Brian Silsbury

During the early 1960s, when we were living in a village in Hertfordshire, United Kingdom, my wife asked me occasionally to drive her to Stevenage, the nearest big town so that she could go shopping. After dropping her off, and agreeing to meet her there a couple of hours later, I drove as quickly as I could to the local railway station. Stevenage station straddles the fastest stretch of railway line between London and the north of England. During the halcyon days of steam locomotion, newly designed and built locomotives were speed tested on this long, straight track. Speed records of 120 miles per hour or more were set and broken from time to time.

I had a passion for steam trains and, whenever possible, loved to spend my time there. When prestigious expresses like the Royal *Scot, Mallard or Coronation Scot* hurtled through the station I got an adrenaline rush.

The harbinger of my first thrill that morning was the loud speaker above my head. It blared, "*Train approaching, stand well back behind the white line.*"

I peered down the track and spotted my favourite locomotive, the Mallard thundering towards me at over 100 miles per hour. Sleek and streamlined, she was the fastest and one of the most beautiful locomotives in England. Cavorting along behind her were nine or ten carriages which rocked and swayed like dancers performing a contemporary ballet.

Nearing the station, she whistles, as if to brag, "I am the *Mallard*, get out of my way."

I stand on the platform and am enveloped by a cacophony of clattering yet sweet sounds and mesmerized by levers, connecting rods, pistons and huge driving wheels, working, straining all in harmony giving the engine driver the speed that he demands.

A symphony of wheel grinding steel, hissing steam, rapid machine-gun firing sounds of wheel on track—clackity-clack.

Then she's gone. I feel a vortex of wind spiral from behind the last carriage and I smell the acrid smoke from the art-deco styled smoke stack. It is heavenly perfume to me.

Unlike the local commuter trains, I never saw the crews of these majestic locomotives gazing or waving out of the side windows. These thoroughbreds demanded that the fireman frantically shovel coal into the boiler's fiery maw, while the engine driver gently caressed and coaxed the best performance out of his fearsome yet beautiful beast.

That morning, standing on the platform, time, like those trains, hurtled by. Before I knew it, my two hours were up and I had to rush back and collect my wife.

(The article was published in the English magazine "Evergreen," Summer 2008).

Kites

By Gerry Atkinson

In the tiny village of Mandena bordering the Marojejy National Park in Madagascar where my son, Paul, is stationed with the Peace Corps, children must devise their own toys. Sardine cans are popular, pulled along behind, or balls made with plastic bags tightly wound with string.

Paul writes,

"The really big craze here is kites. Not the big, elaborated kites on nylon filament floating a mile high in the sky. These are little kites, maybe a foot long, made out of two slivers of bamboo crossed and covered with a piece of old plastic grocery bag, preferably colored: Then you find an old gunnysack and unravel a bunch of strands from it; carefully tie them together with neat little knots until you've got a string about ten feel long. Tie your kite on one end of the string and a long thin stick to the other end. Hold the stick up in the air and run like the wind through the village with the kite trailing behind. Even as I write this, I can see little kites floating back and forth down in the village below my window. All I see are the kites, but I know that beneath those long fluttering spots of color are ragged little barefoot kids, running like the wind up and down the muddy paths."

CURLICUED CLICHES

By Virginia Durbeck

Raise your right hand. Place it over your left shoulder. Pat yourself on the back.

Congratulations for a job well done. Now bring your right hand to your chest and place it over your heart. Feel it? That thump-thump proves your heart is in the right place. With your nose to the grindstone, your ear to the ground, you have beat the odds, and come up smelling like a rose. Lock, stock and barrel, you have survived a mountain out of a molehill.

I'm not going to beat around the bush, but between you and me and the bedpost, the fact of the matter is that day in and day out we face the music, as Father Time is slip-sliding away. We fight tooth and nail, fair and square, fast and furious as we burn the candles at both ends to teach old dogs new tricks. We deserve a feather in our cap fit for a king and a place in the sun for bringing home the bacon, with flying colors, though thick and thin, time after time. When all is said and done, success is measured for better or worse, in the twinkling of an eye.

If you bear the brunt, bury the hatchet, have too many irons in the fire, cook your goose, put the cart before the horse, hang by a thread, hit below the belt and if the die is cast and goes from bad to worse and you're cut to the quick, go on the warpath! Go whole hog, go to the dogs, through hell and high water, hold your head up high. If you have one foot in the grave, if you're rotten to the core and the root of all evil, before you rob Peter to pay Paul, kill the fatted calf plus two birds with one stone, stand on your own two feet and remember: Life is just a bowl of cherries.

When it's high and dry and calm before a storm, out of the blue, in the dead of night, when you least expect it, raindrops keep falling on your head, you can sink or swim when it rains cats and dogs. Keep your chin up when it rains on your parade. Rise and shine! Weather the storm! Every cloud has a silver lining! It's survival of the fittest. Walk on the sunny side of the street, free and easy, dressed to kill, a sight for sore eyes, a thing of beauty and a joy forever. For old times sake, let a smile be your umbrella.

In a nutshell, straight from the horse's mouth, to tell the truth, our tower of strength is peace of mind, patience of Job, having one's cake and eating it, too. Be top dog and to say the least, make a silk purse out of a sow's ear, turn over a new leaf and with tongue in check, swear on a stack of Bibles and live happily ever after.

Things I Remember

By Peggy Hall

Growing up in the 1930s and 40s, or what your grandchildren might call the "olden days," we took many services for granted. Our aging children, don't have a clue what they missed.

First thing that comes to mind is the Helms Bakery truck that drove the neighborhood streets coaxing "stay at home mom's" out of their houses with a toot of his whistle, to purchase bread and pastries.

The milk man delivered milk, cream, and cottage cheese to the back door or the ice box. The Fuller Brush man, ready to give you a free vegetable brush, with hopes you might buy two or more from his display. The iceman, with a large block of ice, carried it to the customer's house where he placed it into the "Ice box". That was before the refrigerator came into being. The rag man was ready to give you a few cents for old rags.

The mailman delivered mail twice a day, six days a week and had special delivery services for those who needed something delivered today, not tomorrow. The Good Humor man drove the neighborhood and beach area streets, playing a little tune that called children out of their homes, with a nickel in hand, ready for a Good Humor ice cream bar. If you were lucky you might find "Good Humor" printed on the stick which entitled you to a free ice cream.

Whether at church or a dark theater, an usher led you to your seat. The few gentlemen who could afford a round of golf had a caddy to carry the clubs and tell you which way to hit the ball. In those "olden days," an elevator operator, in uniform, would actually push the button for the floor you needed. When you entered a shoe store, salesmen measured your feet, brought out the shoe you desired, and slipped it onto your foot.

Most of those services no longer exist. We have learned to do many things for ourselves. Once in awhile I do wish I could see the Fuller Brush man at my front door. I need a new vegetable brush.

.

Why Write?

By Penny De Ley

because I must
must as the child must run
the bird sing.

because I can't hold back the flood
of orange poppies after rain

because the past seeps back
laughter and fear
the angry word
I see my father's face
suddenly know
My heart beats
the pencil writes
I turn the cardboard
tube until the words
fall into place
like bits of colored glass

Yes   Yes

Devotion

By Doris Thome

Borders coffee shop, usually so full of young people whose attentions are focused on their computers, is empty this morning. Empty, that is, except for one elderly couple I estimate to be in their nineties.

What I notice first and cannot walk away from, is the man down on one knee in front of the woman, spooning food into her mouth. Tiny and shriveled, the old woman sits in one of Borders brown club chairs her mouth opening like a baby bird. Her sneakered feet dangle inches off the floor.

The gangly man talks softly to the sweet-lined face under the faded and worn knitted cloche. For a cold day their clothing seems meager. Are they homeless? A blue and white dress, a thin rust shawl, and long white knee socks cover her. His clothing too, short–sleeved shirt, chinos, similar white socks and sandals, appear much too light. The only thing that seems to infer warmth is the man's full and curly, snow-white beard.

I came to shop but cannot walk away. Their sweet natures and caring attention to each other plus the fact they are unaware of anyone else, decides me. I reach for a magazine from the rack and deposit myself near to observe this couple.

How often does one get an opportunity to watch devotion such as this? They share conversation, two powdered-sugar-coated cookies and a cup of coffee. One bit for her, one for him, a gulp of coffee for each. His hand reaches to wipe some powdered sugar from the corner of her mouth.

Food gone, he rises. I see now they do have jackets. Tall and painfully thin, he lifts their garments to sit down in the chair next to hers. Newspaper in hand he reads her the printed words. Blind, she listens as she has done throughout their stay. It is then I notice the wheelchair parked on the other side of his chair. He has wheeled her in, lifted her into the soft comfortable chair, fed her and now reads to her. A heavy lump of emotion sticks in the middle of my chest, and overwhelmed at the level of compassion I bear witness to, I take my voyeuristic self off to make my book purchases. I leave gladdened.

Reflection

"Lady Bug, Lady Bug, fly Away home"

FAMILY

By Sharon Alvarado

She ran out of the house. Using the back of her hands to roughly wipe away tears from her eyes. Small knuckles with hard little bones bruising soft cheeks.

She heard the door slam, a heavy thud shutting out the voices within.

The sun did not seem so bright; she couldn't hear the birds. The day felt different. It felt heavy; yes that was the word, heavy. She could sit down and never get up, but not here, not where they might see her. She took a deep breath and felt her body shudder.

They didn't know she was there, listening. She had heard them before: talking about her mother. She didn't want to hear it any more.

She didn't know what abandon meant but when they called her mother a whore and a pig she knew it was bad. Very bad.

Sometimes they told her she was just like her mother and they used that same voice. The voice that made her want to run away and melt into the floor. It was the voice that made her stomach get tight and told her something was wrong with her. She just didn't know what.

Standing outside it was quiet. She could feel the rough wood of the porch under her feet. She made herself move, across the porch and down the stairs. Moving   toward the large hedge separating the yard from the street. They wouldn't see her behind the hedge.

She would not think about how long it had been since she had seen her mother and father. She really did not want to see them. She decided she did not care. She hated them, she hated them all.

She ran her hand along the hedge. It had purple berries. She felt her fingers slip across the green leaves, gravel and dirt crept between her toes. She looked up to see a beautiful web; a big fat spider at the center. The web reminded her of the doilies her aunt made. They were everywhere in the house. On the arms of the chairs, on the tables.
Stiff white spider webs everywhere. Her aunt spent hours making them.

Slowly she put her finger into the web, pulling.
She watched the spider struggle, the web collapse.

A loud slap, the squishy mess in her hands.
No spider.

No web.

She rubbed her hands slowly on her dress.

Moving away from the hedge she began to sing.

"Lady Bug   Lady Bug
Fly Away Home
Your House is on Fire
Your Children Will Burn"

Labyrinth

By Jeanne Northsinger

precious Earth
water, air and fiery life
your garden spins around me
stones of ages, cracked and
solid remnants of your birth
enclose this circuitous, meandering path

smaller stones, coins or significant articles
still, quiet evidence of others footsteps along this path
prayers left by unknown pilgrims

hot dirt warms my feet through thick shoes
I pause, raise my eyes from the earth
to take in sea and sky
hawk hovers like a kite, soars, dives

breeze first warm then cool
rustle of grass
scent of anise
dog bark
bell

rooster crow

dove coo

another bell

I lift up my heart to take it in

be in the center of the beauty

notice

absorb

forget to finish

there is no destination

A Quonset Hut Village

By Betty Battey

In the spring of 1949 I applied to the Los Angeles School District to teach in the elementary grades. I was hired after taking a written exam, a physical, and filling out a great deal of paper work. I wanted to be assigned to a school in the Los Feliz-Silverlake area of Los Angeles. My appointment was to serve as a first grade teacher at the Rodger Young Village Elementary School. I had never heard of the school and wondered where it was located. I found out it was located in Griffith Park off Riverside Drive.

The Rodger Young School was named after a World War II hero from Ohio who had saved his platoon single-handedly in the Solomon Islands. The school opened in 1946 to serve the nation's largest veteran housing project. The complex was erected by the Los Angeles housing authority to relieve an acute housing shortage created by veterans settling in Southern California following World War II. It was located on 100 acres of a decommissioned National Guard air base located in northeast Griffith Park. The Housing Authority erected 750 surplus Quonset huts to house 1,500 families or about 6,000 residents. The elongated Quonset huts were divided into two private living quarters, each with two bedrooms, a bathroom, and a combined kitchen and living room area. The young housewives were very creative in decorating their Quonset hut homes. They made curtains and bedspreads, and added other special touches to make their quarters attractive.

Rodger Young Village offered many services to the residents. Most of the families did not own an automobile. There was bus service to the park that took residents to other areas of the City of Los Angeles. The village had a grocery store, a variety store, a baby store, a theatre, a malt shop, a library, a playground, a community newspaper, a dentist, and even a bar. Of course a focal point in the community was the Rodger Young Elementary School.

The school consisted of surplus double bungalows placed around an open black top area. There were so many elementary children the school operated on double sessions. There were morning and afternoon sessions requiring a large faculty assigned to either morning or afternoon classes. The classrooms were spacious and had storage cupboards, blackboards, and sinks for painting and clay projects.

Rainy days were hard because there were no halls or covered walkways. Since all the children ate at home no food services were required.

As the years passed housing became available to the veterans and they moved to small tract homes in the San Fernando Valley, Downey, Montebello, and other communities. The village closed in April 1954 and the faculty was assigned to other schools in the Los Angeles district.

Today the acreage is the parking lot for the Los Angeles Zoo.

My Nephew John

By A.L. Quackenbush

My nephew, John, was born July 23, 1950. He was Janet and Phillip's, first born. He was my first born nephew so I considered him special. Others in the family also regarded him as special. He was both his maternal and paternal grandmothers' first grandchild. My brother hailed the arrival of his first nephew born on his birthday. Other family and friends welcomed John's arrival excitedly.

The family enjoyed John during his early years. He was eager to grow and learn. When he started grade school, his teachers marveled at his successes, particularly his artistic flair.

John started high school. After his grade school experience, his family had high hopes for him. But things turned sour during his freshman year. John became quite sullen and angry. His grades fell. He turned away from his family. Janet and Phillip didn't know what to do.

During high school, John went from bad to worse as he became enmeshed in drugs and alcohol. His parent sought help, but John continued his pattern of life. In his senior year he ran away from home and went to Hollywood where the police arrested him for buying drugs. Ultimately, he was shipped home where he was incarcerated in juvenile hall. Soon after, Janet and Phillip were able to obtain John's release. He went home with them, still sullen.

John became incorrigible. No matter what his parents did to try to remedy the situation, John would lash back angrily. When John turned eighteen, he announced that he was moving out. He had found a buddy and they were going to live in an apartment. His parents were concerned, but secretly relieved.

John survived on booze, drugs and pizza which he delivered for Pizza Hut. The years passed and the family knew little about John. He never came home or called except on his birthday when he would appear expecting some sort of gift, especially money. He told them with alcohol on his breath that he didn't "do" drugs anymore.

The years passed. One time John called his mother and told her happily that he was getting married. Janet planned a wedding for him and his bride. The wedding was a happy time and Janet was filled with high hopes. But the marriage lasted only months. Susan couldn't take the alcohol and drugs that permeated their lives.

Life continued the same for John. Booze and drugs dominated his being. Every now and then he would find a job, but it never lasted. Once in awhile he would visit his parents on his birthday.

Many years later when John was in his forties, he became homeless. He relied on public assistance. He never saw his folks. But one day he was so down on his luck, he went to the Rescue Mission. He stayed there for a year taking part in the recovery program. During that time he also contacted his parents. They were ecstatic. John was coming home they thought.

He settled into an apartment and found a job as a graphic artist. He seemed happy and content. But six months later, John lost his job because he had been drinking. He dropped from sight and to this day, Janet and Phillip do not know where he is.

So if you see a drunken middle-aged man out on his luck, it may be John.

Fourth Dimension

By Bob Fisher

You might chase after it and never find it. You might suddenly fall into it without seeking, elusive as it is. Poets clothe it with an air of mystery and try to name sunset and sunrise boundaries.

I wait for the yellow blaze of day to fade into the silver magic of star and moonlight. I go into the mountain night and pass through the edge into the fourth dimension.

My ear opens with increased sensitivity to infinitesimal whisperings, rustlings, murmurings. Cooling night awakes gentle winds to vibrate needles of pine, fronds of cedar. Lungs, bruised by shallow inflation of hot dusty 3rd dimension air now fill deeply with the fragrant coolness of forest filtered night airs.

I start in sudden surprise at the nearly inaudible rustle of a small animal darting through the forest duff. I marvel at the high setting of my awareness. My ears are already turning to a new sound. High lacy murmurs, whisperings. A miniature stream silvering across the forest floor shattering starlight. My footfalls crash miniature earthquakes against the fabric of the night. I stop those noisy steps to savor the absolute quiet of the night.

Silence.   Silence.

Only optical music of the sky.

My ears tune to faint vibrations. Many more steps and the sound intensifies into rushing water. It is closer now. The moon outlines the deep cleft in the mountain wall where the Roaring Fork rushes through a narrow gap in the race to meet King River. Soon the stream is close and I hear voices of rushing water gossiping with the rocks and branches. In a disturbingly human way the sounds translate into cries or calls, even snatches of talk-but imagination returns the sound to white water passing on the tale of the long dash from the high mountain snows. Now there is no single sound intense enough to pierce the roar of falling water. All the keys of the mountain organ are sounding at once and through the cacophony I feel the diapason rumble vibrating in the rock beneath me. I feel and hear this wild dream, full of the magic that moonlight adds to the rush of water. On through the wind driven symphony of night. No longer a dimension of time to dash the extreme full opening of the senses. Ahhh

But at last reluctantly, I move through the edge of the fourth dimension. In wonder at the special night, I thread my way through silent camps and slip into the sleeping bag. One long look at stars flashing through the pine silhouette above. I sleep.

Dark Rider
(The crime you wish you had committed)

By Audrey E. Martinson

Mellowed old ranch house snugged in among the trees. Opens up in front to the narrow country road, bordering a lush rolling golf course. Immaculate as it meanders around the lake. A perfect path. Every evening we walk twice around, the dog's glory in the freedom, the velvety feel beneath their paws. Darkness falls as, satisfied we return to the shabby comfort of our home.

But what is this? My oldest son comes home, angered. He had taken his dog on this favorite walk and been sternly dismissed.

"No more trespassing on the golf course--members only--no disturbing the players" Players? At *night*?? And next week a fence, then a thorny hedge.

The plan forms. As dusk brings soft mist to the lake I don dark jeans, black hooded sweater. Steal down to the stable, where my horse greets me with a soft whicker of surprise. Hanging a lantern on the hook I quickly put on saddle and bridle, rub powdered charcoal on to his wide white blaze, four white stockings.

Swinging into the saddle I ride swiftly up the drive to the golf course, to the entrance we always use for our evening walks. Softly my horse snorts his excitement at this unusual treat, ears twitching, pointing almost touching as he tosses his head, flaxen mane flowing, straining at the bit.

"All right, boy, let's GO!"

Prancing, pivoting, then into a swift canter. Not on the cart path this time, but straight down the immaculate greens, sharp hooves cutting a trail in the soft grass. Wind whistles around us as the canter becomes a gallop, and throwing any caution to the winds, we fly around the course. Over the road, up the hill, never slackening our pace. Pounding hooves cut divots into the grass, plainly marking the trail of our last evening "walk."

Satisfied, I walk my horse back to the stables, rub him down, blanket him for the night.

In the morning the dismayed greens keepers wish they had left well enough alone. The quiet dog walkers, so careful of the environment, what harm had they done?

HITCHHIKING

By Paul Barrett

Were you ever hitchhiking and got stuck at some remote spot and thought you might spend the rest of your life there waiting for a ride?

Well, maybe not. People don't hitchhike much now. Let me tell you my hitchhiking story.

If you look at the map of Nevada, you will notice that the highway leaving Reno travels towards the northeast corner of Nevada and then turns east towards Salt Lake City. At the point where it turns east, there is a junction where a highway takes off to the north. This junction is the locale of my story.

At dusk, I hitched a ride just outside of Reno. It was in an old car and the passenger side window was missing. After riding all night with the cold desert air, I was chilled. When I was deposited at the junction, the warmth of the early morning sun felt good.

The hitchhiking situation looked bad. As I remember, there was a car passing on the east-west highway every five or ten minutes. This was 1943 in the middle of World War II and gasoline rationing had reduced travel. The highway going north to Montana (where I was returning to begin my senior year of college) had a discouraging dribble of traffic.

In this situation a hitchhiker has lots of time to spare. I will tell you how I used my time.

First, I checked out the environment. The sagebrush is a bush about two or three feet tall that has small blue-gray leaves. Sparse rain limits the spacing of the plants to five or six feet (this makes it easy to walk through a sagebrush desert). Between the plants the soil is a light gray and the wind has blown it smooth. Small mounds of dirt collect about the base of the sagebrush. This group of almost evenly spaced plants is the basic unit that creates the sagebrush desert that covers most of Nevada. Many find uninteresting this uniform blue-gray landscape that goes from horizon to horizon. But they have not spent enough time in it to get a "feel" of the desert. If you look carefully, you will see small hills and rock out-cropping that give depth to the scene. There is a subtle grandeur of the sagebrush desert that painters and photographers have tried to capture but seldom, if ever, succeed.

When I was a child growing up in Nevada, I sometimes accompanied my father on his trips around the state. I had come to feel at home in the desert.

When I was eleven, we moved to one of the most beautiful areas in Montana. One night soon after we arrived, I lay in bed and felt homesick for the Nevada desert - and shed a tear or two.

The sameness of the desert makes any foreign object stand out. While walking around – being not too far from my suitcase - I would look for something for diversion. The printing on an old rusty oil can was carefully scanned. On one of these short walks into the desert. I made an exciting discovery that occupied considerable time. Under a sagebrush, I found a piece of paper that had writing on it. Returning to the side of the road, I sat on my suitcase and carefully studied the weathered document with faded blue ink. It was part of a letter – not the first or last page. After reading this page of the letter, I concluded that it was from a young woman and probably written to a boyfriend – a lonesome hitchhiker stranded at this remote junction. I scanned it carefully for any "intimate details" – there were none. The text was just recounting happenings and news about people.

When in possession of a private communication there is a certain responsibility. In addition, I had the sense that there must be some "Code of the Desert" that requires "-what's found in the desert, stays in the desert." I retraced my steps and carefully replaced the piece of paper under the same sagebrush.

About noon, a large black car stopped and I grabbed my suitcase and ran and jumped in – it was headed north and that was all the information I needed. The man driving the car turned out to be uncommunicative – different from most drivers who pick up hitchhikers, they look for someone to talk to. He revealed nothing about himself or where he was going. I began to connect several things – the big black car; a man concealing information; perhaps a New York accent. I had seen enough gangster movies to develop the suspicion that my companion was ... a gangster.

But he was going in my direction and that is what counts when you are hitching.

Crescent City

By Lisa Stathopoulos

She lies abed in muted darkness
a silver swatch of moonlight crawling
unheeded the span of the ceiling.
A luminous glow splays across her pale face.
Roused she strains to hear the hoarse bay
of sea lions perched on rugged sea stacks
oddly comforted by this nocturnal reverie.
Solicitude recedes as the tide returns
to the explosive boisterous sea.
Battery Point lighthouse mourns
its sad song of caution, a weary warning
to dauntless sailors.
Damp cheek to pillow, she awaits
the early morning mist that belies
the advent of the day.

Early Times

"She wondered if the rest of her family was alive"

The Trail of Tears

By Grace Altus

My **great-great grandfather**, Samuel Austin Worcester (1798-1859) has always been a hero to me. An ordained Presbyterian Minister, he represented the seventh generation of ministers and missionaries in his New England family. As far as I can determine, he never had theological doubts but was a literal interpreter of the Bible and quite certain that his role in life was to make the New Testament available to the heathen...in his case the Cherokee Indians of the Southern United States. This is not why he is a hero to me. His heroism arises from his total devotion to that tribe, and to his conviction that if he could translate the New Testament into Cherokee, it could not fail to convert this early American people to The Truth.

He recognized the amazing genius of Sequoia in inventing a written language with a whole new alphabet so that the Cherokee could at last be literate in their own language. He was intimately involved in providing a printing press so that the Cherokee Messenger could be widely distributed and read, and he was deeply devoted to his ambition of translating the gospels into Cherokee.

When the board that financed Protestant clergy first appointed him, he was sent to Tennessee and then Georgia, where the Cherokee nation prospered on ancient Indian territory. He started a school, preached to a small number of converts and other local Protestants, and began to raise a family with his wife Ann. Then began one of the ugliest episodes of U.S. history. The governor of Georgia, responding to the clamor of American citizens seeking homesteads, declared the Cherokees were to be removed from their ancestral lands to the area west of the Mississippi now known as Oklahoma, but then undeveloped and uninviting new lands.

Enter my great-great grandfather's heroism. He vigorously opposed the land grab by Georgia's government and participated in a lawsuit, which went to the Supreme Court, eventually with a verdict in the Cherokees' favor. Despite the verdict, President Jackson and officials in Georgia pursued the Indian exile and sentenced the Reverend Worcester for a term of four years at hard labor. Up to the last moment, he could have been freed by signing an oath of allegiance to Georgia, which nine of his co-defendants did; he and one other protestor declined such a way out. He spent sixteen months incarcerated. He was released to learn that his infant daughter had died and his wife was desperately ill.

FLY-BOYS

By Paul Edwards

I **happened to be based** at a small Naval Air Station in Sanford, Maine during WWII, whose responsibility it was to test aircraft arresting gear which would wind up on carrier decks. While there I received orders to report to the Naval Air Station in Brunswick, Maine, in the north-central part of the state. I was kept in the dark about what my duties were going to be until I got there. It turned out that I was to be attached to a British Corsair Squadron as a liaison officer. That meant that I was to acquire anything that the squadron needed while they were stationed in Brunswick.

It seems that the F4U Corsair planes for their squadron had been acquired through the lend-lease program of the Marshall Plan and the pilots, who had already received their training, had come to Brunswick to prepare themselves for their part in WWII. They had been practicing their ADDLES (that means Aircraft Dummy Deck Landing) for weeks. This was practice for catching the arresting gear on the deck of the aircraft carrier which takes a great deal of precision.

The first skipper and Executive officer of the squadron had met in midair (due to mixed signals) and had killed each other. I had been called in to help hold the squadron together until they acquired a new skipper and Exec to replace them. In addition to being good pilots, these guys were barrels of fun. They would play jokes on one another and were a typical fly-boy group of guys –daring, committed to flying and fun-loving.

In my spare time I called each one aside and drew his caricature. They had a lot of fun kidding each other about their caricatures. Eventually the drawings wound up in what they called a line-book. It was a history of what happened to them as they became a squadron.

Rhodes, West, Forsythe, Wiley and Holland were from New Zealand. The rest were from either Australia or Great Britain. The new skipper, Leftenant Commander Pridham-Whipple was from Great Britain.

Later in the war I heard from a fellow-officer that this squadron was instrumental in knocking off (sinking) the German Pocket battleship, the Von Tirpitz, docked at that time in Alton Fjord, one of the many inlets in Norway.

Memories

By Marge Livingstone

Overnight the world had changed. Viewed from my upstairs bedroom window, the landscape was totally white. Snow covered the bare-limbed cherry trees at the bottom of the hill and shrouded the farm tractor in a shapeless coat. My grandfather's footprints, from house to barn, had crunched deep holes in the snowdrifts. In front of the farmhouse the newly plowed road formed a deep, cold, snow packed passageway. The day held an implicit promise -- no school.

The country community of Bauer, founded in 1850 by four Catholic families of German descent, is set among the hills of southeastern Iowa. Mother and I had recently moved there to my grandfather's farm. Dolores, my new neighbor, was 10 and I, two years younger. We got along well, although I was wary of her mischievous moments.

Sister Serena, principal of our parochial school, kept the rural party line busy as she announced school would be closed until further notice. Dolores and I began to make plans.

For lack of snow, our new sleds had been stored

away since Christmas. Now was our chance to use them. After much discussion we decided on a visit to neighboring Rosemount where Dolores said there lived a woman 100 years old. Bundled in warm clothing, woolen head scarves tied tightly under our chins and feet buckled into galoshes, we set out.

Up the hills we trudged and down we coasted, our sleds' steel blades making a swooshing sound against the snow. As time passed our mittens became soggy, our cheeks cold and red. Finally, Dolores said to me, "We must be in Rosemount by now. Let's stop at the next house. I'm thirsty."

"Okay." I replied.

We could see, at the top of the next hill, a 2-story farmhouse close to the road.

"We'll stop there." said Dolores, "You go up and knock."

"Why don't you," I sputtered. "You've lived here longer than I have."

"But you're younger," she quickly replied, as though that had something to do with it.

At my first knock the door opened. A rotund, jolly looking woman stood in the doorway obviously curious as to why two bedraggled looking children were on her doorstep.

Before I could speak she exclaimed,

"You poor things. You must be frozen. Come in. Get warm. I'll get you some hot cider."

As she led us toward the warmth of a huge stove in the adjoining room, we saw in the corner a small, wizened old lady; her bony hands resting atop a blanket covering her slight form. Her feet, in red carpet slippers, barely touched the floor as she dozed in a high-backed rocking chair. Dolores pushed against my side, gave me a bruising nudge, and whispered in my ear, "That's her. That's the 100 year old woman."

A month ago Dolores came to visit me. The youngest of her four sons, Jimmy, drove her up from Claremont. We had kept in touch with an occasional phone call and cards for special occasions, but had not seen each other for over 10 years. Once settled, we began to catch up on events in our lives. Midpoint in our reminiscing I asked Dolores, "Do you remember sledding to Rosemount to see the 100 year old woman?"

In her familiar, drily humorous manner she replied, "Yes, and she was only 90!"

The Last day of Summer

By Larry Mason

When I was a child, I spoke as a child, I behaved as a child, but when I became a man, I put away childish things.

How often I heard these words in church. Drummed into my head, like some advance warning that things would not always be as they then were. I hated the thought of growing up. Like death, we know it's coming, but we don't face it, don't believe it will really happen to us. Yet we know it will.

Boys Club Camp was the ultimate denial of things to come. Every summer we boarded the bus that took us to our camp on Cicero Creek, singing songs all the way. Mr Gorman, the Camp Director, devised camp lyrics to popular music and it was a celebration of boyhood, like Pinocchio's Pleasure Island without the decadent overtones.

We took our assigned beds in one of eight "Big Ten" cabins, whose open windows, like natural air conditioning, made the Indiana summer nights cold enough for us to snuggle beneath wool blankets. The days were one long romp of softball, volleyball, swimming, fishing, and gorging ourselves on Mrs Gorman's home cooking.

Every night we gathered around a roaring blaze and sang our camp songs, until at last the bonfire fell into glowing embers. The last song of the night was Taps. One of the cabins' occupants would have gone up into the wooded hillside above the quadrangle, and when the last note was sung, they would sing it back down like a faint echo.

Now it's the last night of camp - ever, and I'm huddled around the dying embers with my closest buddies, Jack and Wayne, Paul and Dave. Tomorrow we'll pile into the bus and head back to the hot, noisy city, where we'll take up a new phase of our lives - high school, then college and gradually adulthood will open and boyhood will close behind us. Gone will be the endless days of summer - fishing, swimming day after day, baseball, and those magical nights: kick the can; hunting night crawlers for tomorrow's bait; filling jars with "lightning bugs." Halloween came with its outrageous costumes and scary shadows, where werewolves lurked behind every bush and Frankenstein stomped stiff-legged behind us- arms outstretched; and where, when the urge hit us, we sent rivulets down the sidewalks that looked for all the world like those maps of the Mississippi that hung in our classrooms. Tomorrow we will begin to put away childish things.

But for now we savor boyhood's last moments as we wait for the echo to come down from the hills. All is quiet except for the crackle of the dying embers. Even the crickets seem to have grown silent. Then it comes, so faint we strain to hear it:

Day is done, Gone the sun, From the hills from the lakes, from the sky,

As if on cue, the moon clears the treetops beyond Cicero, bathing us in an ivory glow that will etch this moment in my memory for a lifetime.

All is well, safely rest, God is nigh.

Doing Without

By Ruby Buck

Key West, Florida was a sleepy little fishing town in 1955 and 1956. Stately palm trees lined the narrow streets, while bright red bougainvillea bloomed in every garden. Abundant sunshine and balmy weather added to its charm.

I am sure Hemingway could not have written "Old Man and the Sea" any place else.

Fishing was the main source of income in Key West; the United States Navy was second. My husband was stationed on one of the staffs there and the family, consisting of our two sons, Manor 6 and Fred 4 and us settled into navy housing on a man-made island close to Key West.

No matter where you lived in the area, you could practically fish from your backyard. We were able to do just that at the waters edge about 100 feet from our back door.

My husband, Beau, bought a small motorboat so he and Manor could go fishing. They also fashioned a fishing pole from a broomstick, some string and a hook. When the pole was not in use, it was securely placed behind a door out of harms way with an admonition, "Do not touch."

Beau and I really loved to sleep late on Sunday mornings and the boys were awfully good about keeping quiet and entertaining themselves. Doing without sleep is the price you pay for having children. You never seem to catch up.

About ten o'clock one Sunday morning, we heard a tapping on our bedroom door. Manor was standing there mumbling.

"Fred hurt his mouth with the pole." Hearing Fred crying, we ran into the living room where we found him with blood oozing from his mouth and the barb of the fishhook embedded in his lip. He was so scared his big blue eyes were twice their normal size.

We jumped into some clothes and drove to the navy dispensary about ten minutes from the house.

The Doctor took us into the emergency room. He smiled and said, "I've seen lots of fish in Key West, but this one is the biggest."

In our haste to get to the hospital, neither one of us thought to cut the string from the pole. When we took time to really look, there was poor Fred, with broom handle, string and hook, all hanging from his bottom lip.

The doctor cut the string away, then cut the hook in two and pushed the barb through and out the lip.

After this incident, we didn't sleep late for many, many years.

A Christmas Card to the Red Cross

By Bill Livingstone

The frigid air was crystal clear outside the
shuttered barracks windows and the full winter moon
glistened off the hard-packed snow. In the dim light
from the guard tower a German guard patrolling the
perimeter fence pulled the collar of his great coat
tighter around his shoulders. His big guard dog
strained against his leash, anxious to get back to the
relative warmth of its kennel.

The guard could hear the voices of hundreds of
men inside the barracks singing Christmas carols. The
Christian melodies were familiar to him, but the words
were not. This was because the words were English.
The carols were sung by American Prisoners of War.

It was Christmas Eve, 1944, and the snow had
been on the ground for several weeks at Stalag Luft IV,
located near what is now Stettin Poland, a few miles
from the Baltic Sea. Our prison camp was composed
of four double barbed wire fenced compounds, with a
guard tower located about every 200 feet along the
fence lines. In each compound there were ten large
barrack buildings with ten rooms in each barrack.

There were usually about 25 men living in each of the 25-foot-square rooms with enough built-in double-deck bunks for everyone. The bunks had straw mattresses and each man had one German Army blanket. In wintertime we went to bed fully clothed.

At the prisoner count in the compound that morning a German officer announced in his broken English, "The Germany people honor the tradition of Christmas, and we respect your desire to celebrate this day in your traditional manner as best you can. Therefore, the guards will take a number of you into the forest this morning to cut and bring back a Christmas tree for each room in the camp."

For about a week now the POWs had been talking about Christmas, thinking of their loved ones at home, and preparing for some sort of celebration -- at least recognition of the fact that it was a special day.

Our room leader, Murph, suggested, "Whata ya say we get a full chocolate ration from each guy in the room, melt it down, and mix it with some dried fruit and crumbled graham crackers and cookies, and make a sort of chocolate cake for Christmas?"

He got responses like, "Sounds good to me." "Great idea" and "Let's do it!"

If this sounds like POWs in Germany during WW II had it made -- well perhaps. And the reason: The Red Cross. The ingredients we used to make our "Christmas Cake" came from the food parcels we received each week from the Red Cross. They were trucked into Germany by the International Red Cross through Switzerland, a neutral country.

At Stalag Luft IV we essentially got two kinds of food: The American Red Cross American food parcels and German food cooked in the camp's central kitchen. The Red Cross food came in corrugated boxes about a foot square and six inches high. The ten pound food parcels provided minimum nourishment for one man for one week.

Almost all the Red Cross food could be eaten "as is," or could be cooked if heat was available. For example there was good old canned Spam, beef stew, cheese, powdered milk, dried fruit, something called "reconstituted butter," some kind of crackers or cookies, a small bar of "Swan" soap, and that all-time favorite, a quarter pound bar of Hershey's sweet chocolate.

Two packages of cigarettes were also included in each Red Cross parcel. Everything in the parcels was traded among the prisoners with all items valued in packs of cigarettes. Spam and the chocolate bar, for example, were each worth three packs, beef stew was worth two, and prunes and cheese worth one each. For us non-smokers this was a bonanza.

One time I heard a guy yell down the central corridor of the barrack, "Anyone want to trade prunes for cheese?" So you see they had medicinal qualities too.

After the seven o'clock prisoner count in front of the barracks each morning, we cooked our own breakfast on the potbellied stove in our room. This took a while because the top of the stove was only about a foot in diameter, and everyone wanted to use it. Breakfast was usually a slice of fried Spam and a slice of German black bread toasted on the stove top with the butter that came in the Red Cross parcels. The German bread had straw in it and heaven knows what else. Sawdust, I guess. Lunch was something else out of the Red Cross parcel.

Dinner was German food and was usually some kind of soup. It was cooked by KPs in a central kitchen and brought to us in our room. My first meal at Stalag Luft IV was what we jokingly called "ball bearing" soup because it was made of garbanzo-like beans which were quite hard. It was my first hot meal in a while so it smelled and tasted good to me. I commented to one on my new buddies, "Hey, this soup ain't half bad."

"It would be a lot better without the weevils," he replied.

"Weevils?"

"Yeah. Open up one of those beans and have a look".

So I got one onto my spoon and cut it open with my knife (table knives were permitted). Sure enough, a little black guy about an eighth of an inch in diameter. And every bean had one. After a while one didn't think about it anymore.

No one was getting fat on the diet at Stalag Luft IV, but we ate well compared to political and Russian POWs who got no Red Cross food parcels. Those of us who went to chapel thanked God, and those who didn't, I'm sure, at least thanked their lucky stars, that the Red Cross was there when we needed them most. Coffee and donuts at troop train stops were nice, but Red Cross food parcels in Allied POW camps all across Germany were a blessing.

On this Christmas Eve in 1944 the rooms at Stalag Luft IV smelled of evergreens -- an aroma that took us back to our homes and families. There was nothing to decorate the trees from the nearby woods;

paper was in very short supply. We didn't exchange gifts because it was simply impractical, but we sang Christmas carols and played games. Something called "red dog" and gin rummy were most popular.

"Lights out" was to be at midnight on Christmas Eve instead of the usual nine o'clock" The extension to midnight, alone, was reason for celebration. Of course we were all locked in the barracks an hour before sundown everyday, including Christmas Eve.

By nine o'clock we were ready for our "chocolate cake," and everyone gathered around the table in the center of the room to get their share. With a great flourish Murph cut into our first cake since capture. He managed to get 24 pieces of approximately the same size and handed them out.

It was a strange, almost ethereal moment when we all took a bite of our cake -- we suddenly realized, this was it. This was it for the Christmas of 1944. This was the opening of Christmas gifts at home. This was our Christmas turkey, goose, or ham dinner with family gathered round. This was the moment of love for our moms, dads, sisters, brothers, and sweethearts. We were all sure we would be with them by next Christmas, but we also knew that this bittersweet moment would live in our memories forever.

Merry Christmas, Red Cross. May your pursuit of peace on earth and good will toward man from 1945 to 2011, endure forever.

Early Times – Hannah Dustin

By Priscilla Boyan

Hannah had been in labor for nineteen hours but it seemed like ninety. Mary Neff, her nearest neighbor, a dear friend and also a nurse, leaned over and wiped the sweat from Hannah's brow.

The year was 1697 and Hannah Dustin, age 40, was birthing her thirteenth child. The others had come relatively easy. Why was this one taking so long? Hannah shivered with an already-approaching fever. Mary massaged her abdomen and whispered, "good, good!" Hannah pushed hard, relaxed and pushed hard again. Little Martha Dustin slid into Mary's waiting arms and promptly wailed in protest at having been forced from the warm haven of her mother's womb.

It was March and there was still snow on the ground outside the cabin. New England was not ready yet for spring. Thomas, Hannah's husband, had taken the six younger children into Haverhill, Massachusetts to stay with relatives. While their mother was bringing into the world another sibling for them to play with, the older children were doing chores and trying to stay out of the way.

Mary wiped the baby carefully, wrapped her well in the home-spun blanket and placed her in the cradle by the hearth. It was obvious she could not be given to her mother. Hannah was unconscious! Mary rubbed her wrists briskly and called her name. "Hannah, Hannah, wake up and see the wee one. She's beautiful, she's here, it's over." Hannah's eyes flickered and opened briefly and then closed again. It was clear that she was very ill. Mary knew what it was. She had seen it many times – childbed fever. There were some bad days ahead.

Hannah was still in bed following the birth of her baby who Mary Neff had nursed lovingly for six long days. The fever was gone but Hannah was very weak. Thomas, her husband, had managed the other children all week, keeping them occupied and fed.

The morning of March 15, 1697 began as usual. In the small settlement outside Haverhill, where the Dunstins lived, there were five other homesteads, about forty settlers in all. Since his wife was feeling better, Thomas decided to go into Haverhill with all the children to get supplies. The cabin would be quiet for a few hours and when they returned, maybe Hannah and the baby could sit in the rocker by the window and watch the older children shuck corn for supper. Mary was going to bake bread and tidy up the cabin.

After her husband left, Hannah fed the baby, tucked her under one arm and fell asleep. She woke with a start and sensed that something was wrong. Mary, too, was alarmed and went to the window. She peered toward the woods outside. Something moved briefly behind a tree. She gasped and quickly pulled the shade. It was deathly quiet both inside and outside the cabin. They both smelled smoke.

Hannah forced herself to get out of bed. She immediately fell to the floor but struggled up and gestured to Mary to get the baby. Both women knew, without a word being spoken, what was happening; An Indian raid.

In the next moment three Indians burst through the door. Short, stocky, broad shouldered, each was armed with a tomahawk and knife. One of them pushed Mary who was clutching the baby out of the house and a short distance away. Suddenly he snatched the baby from her arms, raised it by its heels and bashed the tiny head against a tree, killing it instantly. Hannah, witnessing this from the doorway, screamed and ran toward her baby, but was grabbed by one of the Indians and thrown over one of the ponies nearby. Mary was quickly hoisted onto another pony. The Indians leaped up behind the women and they took off through the woods which were now on fire.

The first day after their capture Hannah and Mary were kept on the ponies. After that, they were forced to walk even though Hannah could barely keep up. Her grief over her baby's death and the way it had occurred overwhelmed her. She wondered if the rest of her family was alive. She and Mary both feared that their entire settlement was now gone and that many more were captive like themselves. They were fed very little and at night they huddled together, sharing only one blanket, the ground hard and cold beneath their bodies. Occasionally they were put on the ponies for brief periods but mostly they walked.

After several days they reached the Merrimac River and were taken by canoe to an island. Landing, they were handed over to an Indian family living there which was temporarily separated from the other members of the tribe. The family consisted of two men, three women and several younger people. Oddly one of the latter was blond and blue-eyed. Although he was dressed like the others, it was clear that he was not an Indian. He smiled shyly at the two women prisoners. Mary spoke to him. "Do you speak English?"

"Yes," he said, "my name is Samuel Lennurdson."

One of the Indian women poked him with a stick, grunted something, and the boy ducked his head and left the tent.

The next day Hannah learned that Samuel had been with the tribe a year and had learned much of their language. An English boy, seventeen years old, he was soon to become very close to Hannah and Mary. Each of the women had a son about his age. When the chance came, Hannah and Mary shared their story with him.

He was very sympathetic and told them what he had learned about their future. Soon they would leave the island and travel to another Indian village. When they arrived, they would be stripped and made to run the gauntlet. "You will have to run between two rows of savage Indians and they will hit you with all manner of sticks and rocks. It will surely do you in, Mams. I cannot bear to think of it." Hannah and Mary shivered at these words. It was then that the two women and the boy started to hatch a plan for escape.

Although Hannah and Mary had never in their entire lives thought themselves capable of violence, they listened carefully as Samuel continued with instructions. One of the Indians had once told him where to strike a person to kill him very quickly. He passed this knowledge to the women. He also found the hatchets for the deed. Hannah had to think only of her murdered baby, her other children and her husband. She prayed they were still in Haverhill. Mary, a caregiver all her life, but a widow with three children shrugged off the task ahead and prepared to do what was necessary.

Early on the last day of March, 1697 and before dawn, the three captives silently and swiftly attacked the Indians as they slept. Hannah killed the one who had so brutally dashed her newborn baby against the tree. All ten Indians were scalped. One wounded squaw was left alive. Hannah placed the scalps in her shift and wrapped them tightly. The bundle was placed in a canoe and with a few provisions, they left.

History records that after many days, they reached Haverhill and that Hannah was reunited with her husband and children. She, Mary and Samuel became well known New England heroes.

A monument is erected in the center of Haverhill commemorating the terrible ordeal Hanna Dustin endured when she was captured by Indians in March of 1697 at the age of 40. She was one of my ancestors.

Today, traveling by car, you can drive from Haverhill to the place Hannah was taken in about one hour.

WAR TIME ELASTIC

By Doris Wells Miller

It was in the middle of WWII and everyone was making do for the war effort. I was in junior high school and lived almost two miles away. I had to walk because mother could not drive and I did not have enough money to take the bus. It was a bitter cold morning, under 0° so I was bundled up; galoshes, leggings, heavy coat, mittens, scarf and babushka. I was halfway to school when the elastic in my underpants broke. Elastic was one of the items that used substitutes. When my underpants dropped into my leggings they caused a constriction so I could only move a few inches with each step.

I had to make a decision, go home and change or continue. Going home would cause me to be at least an hour late to school and would mean I would have to walk back almost a mile, change clothes, and then walk another two miles to school. Or, I could continue to walk to school and take off the underpants when I arrived and throw them away. Either way I had to walk a mile in my constricted underwear so I decided to continue to school one tiny step at a time.

Hometown Characters
(And you thought the city was bad)

By Joyce Metz

I'd like you to meet some of the folks from my hometown, Lyons, N.Y. Lyons is a small village of 3500 souls situated in upstate New York. By upstate I mean really upstate, not what today's newspapers refer to as upstate. A headline might read, "Upstate Village Besieged by Rats." While reading the article you discover their upstate is 25 miles north of New York City. No, the real upstate is hundreds of miles from NYC. It covers an area from Buffalo to Albany. That's upstate.

Lyons is strategically situated on the banks of the Erie Canal and also next to the N.Y. Central Railroad. This made for a bustling little community offering full employment and plenty of booze. At one time Lyons boasted more saloons per capita than any other place in New York State. Yes, working on the canal or the railroad was thirsty work. Perhaps that is why my stories of Lyons folks involve so much alcohol.

I'll first introduce you to Mose, not Moses. Old Mose could lead no one nowhere. Mose was married and retired. When he had been employed he frequented many of the local drinking establishments after work. Now that he was older he didn't get out much any more so his pals would visit Mose while his wife was at work. They would play cards and, of course, drink. His best friend was Albert, known to imbibe more than Mose.

One day after work, Mose's wife returned home to find him seated at the kitchen table crying.

"Why Mose, whatever is the matter?"

Mose sobbed, "It's Albert. He promised to come see me today and he never showed up."

"Why you damn fool, he's right there."

"Where?" asked Mose, looking around.

"Right there under the table."

Serendipity

"__divine intervention or just plain dumb luck?"

Chance Meeting

By Anne Cushing Cotton

A coyote preceded me on my walk yesterday,
slowing when I slowed,
picking up its pace when I did.
We parted company when it chose
to follow the horse trail that climbs the hill
and finally disappear into the forest.

It never let me get too close, never moved
more that a few yards off. I descried
the markings on its glossy, red-brown coat,
admired the huge ears, tall slinky legs.
What a long Roman nose a coyote has!
I would not care to be a pygmy rabbit
in the vicinity of such a creature.

An adult human of normal size,
I was free to admire it and imagine
we were companions on this heavenly day,
as it sauntered along
pretending ignorance of me, enjoying
the spring weather (perhaps), intent
on its own mysterious purposes.

Lunch at Tupelo's

By Beth Thompson

Late morning on a sunny Santa Barbara day, I'm on my way to lunch with friends at Tupelo Junction. I pass Chicken Little, a children's store. Chicken Little is an inviting shopping mecca where many a grandmother and baby shower guest drop a bundle on toys, accessories and clothing for kids and infants, Scoop is next. Scoop is a gelato shop that advertises its gelato has far less fat than ordinary ice cream. Yummy! No ads comparing amounts of sugar, however.

As I walk by Celadon House, one of my favorite home furnishing places in Santa Barbara, I can't help but notice a lady in the window. Who is she? She looks vaguely familiar. Discreetly, I peer in. Her chin slopes down her neck, not taut like mine. I see rivers of wrinkles banding her neck like the brass ringed women of the Kayan Lahwi tribe of Thailand. Who is this lady? I observe deep etched "smile lines" parenthesizing her mouth and ample crows' feet tracking from the corners of her eyes.

My gaze travels downwards. Should I tell her about the benefits of Victoria Secret's Wonder Bra?

Then I notice the Coldwater Creek drawstring tie twill pants...gain a size...just loosen those cotton ties. She's also wearing a Chico's jacket that many retired ladies of a certain age, sport. I shake my head in disbelief.

What ever happened to that cute forty year old gal? Size 8 in GAP khakis, size 6 Banana Republic Oxford cotton shirt? Where is she?

Think I'll order a Bloody Mary with my fried chicken salad at Tupelo's.

Dreams Realized

By Joan Jacobs

I was born from a clarinet in a bistro in New Orleans. Only a small audience heard me. When I could, I left, because I know I am meant to be heard on a much grander scale.

For the first time, I smell fresh air and see daylight. I am invigorated. I know I can find a big theater where I will be heard by thousands. I wind my way down the street. I float in and out of buildings, around lampposts, around corners. I find cafes and restaurants not much bigger than the bistro I came from. But no big theater.

I'm depressed. I'm starting to lose my tone. I stop to rest outside a bistro, when a note from a tenor sax comes up beside me.

"What are you doing?" he asks.

"I'm looking for a big hall where I can be heard by thousands and thousands."

"You won't find such a place here in New Orleans," he tells me.

"Where can I find one?"

"New York City. I'm heading there myself. Why

don't you join me?

The clarinet and the tenor sax notes hitch a ride on an air current. It carries them miles and miles away from New Orleans. They are in the air for such a long time, that, when they land, they think they are in New York City. As they wind their way down the streets, they meet a note from a drum and a note from a bass viol.

"We're looking for a great hall where we will be heard by thousands and thousands," the clarinet and tenor sax notes tell their new friends.

"You won't find a hall like that here in Memphis. We're going to New York City where we've heard there's such a hall. You're welcome to join us."

While riding on the air current, each note begins to hum. To each note's surprise, they realize they make beautiful music together. Something is lacking, though. They aren't sure what.

At long last, they reach New York City. They begin to wind their way down the street looking for a great hall. Outside a cafe, they run into a note from a trumpet.

"What brings you to New York?" the trumpet asks.

"We're looking for a great hall where we can be

heard by thousands and thousands," the clarinet note tells the trumpet note.

"Follow me," says the trumpet. "I know just the place."

In the distance, they hear a sad, lonely sound. They follow the sound until they come upon a great auditorium. The melancholy note from the piano beckons them inside.

"Why are all of you here?" the piano asks.

"We're looking for a great hall where we can be heard by thousands and thousands," the notes tell the piano.

"This is Carnegie Hall. This great hall can hold thousands and thousands of people."

The piano note begins to hum and the notes from the clarinet, tenor sax, drum, trumpet and bass viol begin to hum along. The trumpet and the piano notes are what the clarinet, tenor sax, drum and bass viol now know was lacking when there was only the four of them.

The next night, thousands and thousands hear the notes perform. They are overwhelmed with the applause and the standing ovation they receive.

Their dreams have come true.

Harry Meets High Society

By Gerson Kumin

It was 1932 and Harry was happy. He was newly graduated from college with a degree in biology and he had gotten a job at the Wood's Hole Oceanographic Institute on Cape Cod.

One weekend he was rowing along, sightseeing, and dreaming about the wealthy families such as the Forbes family who owned some of the properties on the shore. Suddenly he found himself caught in a fast current that was going the wrong way.

Harry rowed hard against the current. As the sweat rolled down he suddenly heard a horn honk behind him. Twisting his head around gave Harry a glimpse of a large yacht that was overtaking him.

"Where are you headed?"

"Woods Hole," he replied.

"Come aboard and we will tow your boat there."

Harry boarded the yacht and was led to the aft section. There was no socializing. He and his boat were returned to Woods Hole and he was left wondering who his rescuers were.

Seventy-seven years were to pass before Harry was to learn the answer. By that time he was in his twilight years. One evening as he was watching a Public Television show he saw the yacht! The show was a history of the Kennedy family. The yacht was tied up at Hyannis port where the Kennedys had a summer home.

At long last Harry knew that somewhere in the depth of time, he had been rescued by a Kennedy.

Oberon

By Larry Mason

On my first day of school, I was prepared. As the youngest of four boys, I was subjected to frequent hazing but was also the beneficiary of my older brothers past experience. Sometimes it was hard to tell the difference. But they provided me with much useful insight, particularly in school, where they had already had the same teachers and always knew what their individual whims were. For the First Grade, they knew Mrs Nackenhorst always asked if anyone knew his abc's. If you did, you had a special place.

Beginning weeks before I started in early January, I was drilled by my brothers on abcdefg - hijklmnop-qrs-tuv- w-x-y-z, with that rhythm, a pause and breath at every dash, until I had it down cold. When Mrs Nackenhorst asked her perennial question, I was surprised that I was the only one who raised his hand. Of course I rattled it off with aplomb, and she rewarded me with a front row corner seat and the title of King of the Fairies. We were still innocent and naive, so it was a regal title.

Over the next few days, Mrs Nackenhorst divided the class into three separate but allegedly equal groups: the Fairies, the Brownies, and the Elves, based on her observation of our academic skills. Though she assured us that all groups were equal, even as First Graders we knew that some were more equal then others, and the Fairies were the elitists. We occupied the front tables, finished our work first, and raised our hands most often. We were altogether insufferable.

I shared the front left-hand table with Harry Shaner, who, while every bit as bright, lacked my assertiveness and was never able to surmount my abc lead. And so my titular head seemed more than secure, except for my less than perfect deportment, a perennial problem with me. I had one tardy (far worse than an absence), and one after school punishment for dancing an impromptu jig while waiting in line for the dismissal bell. Mrs Nackenhorst shook me and sat me down until everybody else had gone. She made me vow I would never engage in such frivolous behavior again. Spontaneity was a threat to a system designed to ingrain conformity and discipline.

So I was already on thin ice one day when I had a little embarrassing accident. We were trained - supposedly - to raise our hands and ask to be excused when the urge hit us, which was frequent with me. For some reason - perhaps I had exceeded my allowed limit - or maybe because I felt immune from detection in my navy blue cords - I let loose. Years later I would laugh at the workplace signs that read:

"Doing a good job around here is like peeing in a pair of dark pants - it gives you a warm feeling, but nobody notices."

It did indeed give me a warm feeling, but Mrs Nackenhorst noticed. But in my blue cords, she didn't notice it was me. She first asked for a confession, then, failing that, she lined all the boys up in the front of the room (girls were always exempt). She then passed in review giving us the sniff test. As she approached our end of the line, Harry reached over, patted the dry side of my pants and announced boldly:

"Nope, it wasn't you."

Thus dissuaded, Mrs Nackenhorst terminated her inspection and my position was secure. For many years, I felt saved by Harry miraculously checking the dry side. Now I wonder - did he know it was me and only wanted to save my butt so he wouldn't have to be King of the Fairies? Or was he just being a loyal subject?

Maybe he just did it out of basic friendship. That's what I would like to think. Screw the King of the Fairies.

Lost In the Desert

By Helen Barron-Liebel

I **checked my watch** as I turned into the entrance to the Palm Springs Airport. We were right on time to meet daughter, Nancy and grandson, Christopher, who were flying in from San Francisco. The plane landed and I watched them disembarking. Christopher, who couldn't even walk the last time I had seen him, ran to my outstretched arms. Hugs all around. We managed to pick up the baggage and the car seat and tuck everyone in, and were soon on our way home to our Palm Springs house.

When daughters and mothers get together after a long absence there seems so much catching up to do. Nancy said she needed to find a speech therapist for Christopher. Already past two he hadn't said a word.

"Oh, don't worry I tried to comfort Nancy. You know with his sister, 9 years older, she probably answers for him before he has a chance."

"No, mother, I am sure there is something wrong."

Concentrating on our conversation, I had missed our turn-off and suddenly everything was dark. No road signs anywhere, no lights, not even a moon or stars. Blowing sand seemed to be covering the road to make driving hazardous. I couldn't be sure in which direction I was traveling. "I'm lost", I blurted out.

From the backseat: "Oh, God."

Nancy said, "I guess I won't need the speech therapist after all."

Luck

By Allen Zimmer

So many years ago but I can still remember that blistering smoggy September day in the San Fernando Valley. Monday morning, eight o'clock sharp, I didn't want to be late to my first job since college and the Air Force. I'd put on my suit and tie, and had my drafting tools in an old tackle box. But when I got there the front door it was locked. Above the door it said Neil Black Architect, but no business hours. He's a professional, so I guessed he opens at nine.

To kill some time, I drove a couple of blocks over to Bob's Big Boy. I grew up only a mile from there and I remembered all the nights tooling through the drive-in, looking for action.

I got a cup of coffee and the *Times* and thought about the craziness of the past two weeks. Planning for the wedding, then driving down here, scouting around for a job. Finally landing one, and then three days ago, rushing back to SLO for the wedding. Then yesterday, our brief honeymoon.

It was a little awkward having to stay with Mom, but we'd get our own place just as soon as I got some money together.

Quarter to nine, so I went back.

This time the door was open. I walked into the drafting room, eight boards, each one occupied. Hum, where was I going to sit? Neil Black was bent over a board talking to a draftsman. He turned and looked at me blankly. I said "hello," gave him my name, and explained "you told me I was starting this morning."

He just stared at me, paused, and finally said. "We open at eight-thirty, ...you're late," and then "....you're fired."

I muttered "but I was here at eight but the door was...." I couldn't finish, he walked back to his office, closing the door behind him. All the draftsmen sat there, silently staring at me. Humiliated, I could only turn and retreat to my VW.

I sat there, helpless; here I am, no job, no money, no place to live, a new bride, and a baby due in 6 months.

I glanced over at the *Times,* picked it up and hopefully turned to the help wanted ads. There were a few listings for architectural drafting, but they had 'license required', or 'experienced only'. There was one I qualified for, but it was up in Santa Barbara.

All I knew about the place was that it's pretty, but architecturally a little backward. I wondered, will I have a future in such a small town. But then, what choice did I have. So I went to the corner 'Flying A' station, stuck a dime in the phone, dialed zero, asked for the long distance operator and gave her the number.

I had the interview the next day. Two days later I was hired.

Was it divine intervention or just plain dumb luck?

Whatever it was, it was the beginning of a wonderful career, in a wonderful city.

Seeing Stars
IN 1985

By Ruby Buck

"**I'll be leaving for the Arctic** next month and
on this trip the top man in the Navy CNO (Chief of
Naval Operations), Admiral James Watkins, will be
visiting our ice station *Crystal* on an inspection tour.
He will be arriving in our company plane. After the
inspection, the submarine *Trepang* will pick him up,
then go to the North Pole. When work is done at the
pole, he will come back to *Crystal* on the sub, and,
we'll fly him back to Thule, Greenland. He will have a
group of fifteen with him, including several
photographers," Beau said.

"Why are you going into chapter and verse
about this trip? This will be your *35th* trip to the
Arctic and you never go into who is coming or going,
so why now?"

"This will be the first time a Chief of Naval
Operations, will have visited an ice camp in the
Arctic, so yeah, this is 'something special.' I
thought that a special balaclava with stars
designating his rank, would be a nice touch ... a
friendly gift. Plus, he can well use it in the cold we will

be expecting in March, which can get down to *30* or 40 below zero. Would you get some stars and sew them on?"

"OK, I'll do it, but now I'd like to ask you some questions."

"Ask away."

"When the submarine reaches Crystal, will it surface?"

"Yes. The admiral and his party will probably use the hatch in the conning tower to come and go if the ice there is over a couple of feet thick. Won't know that until it happens though. Other hatches in the sub can be used if the ice is thin enough."

"I understand, I think. When the *Trepang* gets to the North Pole, will it surface?"

"Every U.S. sub that has gone even near the pole has surfaced. It's a crew morale thing. The sailors usually get out on the ice and play baseball or football, just to say they have done it. They even do it in the winter when it is completely dark ... using lights. I have a photo of a sub doing that. After playing around at the Pole they'll resubmerge and come back to *Crystal*, and we will put the VIPs in the Tri-Turbo and take them back to Greenland."

Satisfied with the who, what, when, and why, I went to a craft shop to find out the how of my mission. I found stars and carefully sewed four of them to the balaclava. With each star sewn, I felt pretty darn patriotic. I knew Beau would be pleased, and the Admiral too. That evening, I showed my handiwork to Beau and his blue eyes took on the dimensions of two saucers. After he stopped laughing, he said, "You can't do that — you just can't."

"Can't do what? What is it I can't do for heavens sake?" The stars are aligned just the way you told me. Can't do what? I don't understand."

"Those are *red* stars. To our military, 'red star' means the USSR. A Russian sub, a ship, an aircraft ... is a 'red star.' Now, can you imagine the highest-ranking officer in the U.S. Navy wearing red stars on his headgear? I'm sure he would prefer loosing both ears and his nose to frostbite than be caught with such a hat."

"Sorry about that. I didn't know all that about those damn red stars. Well, back to the drawing board," I replied.

Fortunately, I was able to find four proper white stars. I removed the red ones and replaced them, but by this time my pride and patriotism had taken a tumble.

Six weeks later, Beau returned to Santa Barbara. He told me that not only was the trip successful, but the balaclava was as well. Admiral Watkins had even invited him to have a cup of coffee on the submarine, and I had a story to write for class.

Balaclava - a close fitting woolen cap that covers the head, neck and tops of the shoulders-holes for eyes-nose.

Conning tower — a raised, enclosed observation post in a submarine, often used as a means of entrance and exit.

Insight

"Count me a believer."

Noah's Daughter

By Penny De Ley

The Lord said to Noah, "I will make a covenant with you, and you shall go into the ark, you and your sons, your wife and your sons' wives with you."

Damn you! Damn you. I can still see you out there, rocking in the waves. May you spend your life puking.

You sent me out to gather wild joogas, and I ran joyously, knowing how much you love them. I sought the best trees, reached way in, didn't mind the thorns scratching my face or sap sticking to my hands. I chose the fruits just coming on ripe, still firm at the stem end, the blossom end near bursting with sweet. I plucked only ones the birds had not pecked at. My basket heaped like a breast, I ran for home. When the rain came on, I didn't care that my soaked skirt clung to my legs or my hair hung wet and heavy around my neck. In my mind I pictured your smile, saw you reach out, bring one to your mouth. And with the juice dripping down your beard you would say, "These are good."

But you had left! No, you didn't forget me. You

might have, except for the joogas you so love. You tricked me, were even willing to sacrifice your favorite fruit so as not to take me with you. Am I so ugly, so deformed that you had no room for me? There was room enough for my brother Ham--and his wife. For Japheth and his bride you built a separate compartment. And Shem, who also brought a wife, when you die, he will be head of the family.

Is it because of your rule about taking two of everything, two jackals, two rams, two camels? Is it because there is only one of me, because the man you chose for me took one look and walked to another village?

Or is it because I use my head and speak my piece? Is it because your God, this Yahweh you worship, demands that women must remain silent, that they should have a mouth only between their legs? Well let me tell you this (may my words have wings), I shall have sisters. No, not from your loins, nor from your sons, nor your son's sons. But they will come. And they will think and speak their minds, and their men will hear them.

As for you, I shall prophesy: one of your sons shall see you naked and know you for what you are. Oh God...Oh God. I am not crying because I am a woman; I am not weak. I'm crying because I loved you. And I wanted so much for you to love me.

Ticonderoga # 2 Soft

By Beth Thompson

Had my annual mammogram today. My heart races, palms sweat, butterflies dance in my stomach as I wait in a charming hospital gown which opens in front. It's interesting how I let my breasts define me. When I was younger I always wished my boobs were fuller, bigger... size C at least. As I matured I came to terms with my breasts and appreciated their perkiness, thrusting upward and smiling at the world. I was proud of them. They were petite like me. My husband used to tease me and say that when I was older I wouldn't be able to pass "The Pencil Test." That's when you place a pencil underneath your breast and if your breast is upright, the pencil will fall to the ground. I'd laugh and say, "No, that will never happen to me!"

When I was nursing my sons my breasts grew to melon size. They resembled silicone implants. I was embarrassed by their hugeness but my husband loved their milky fullness. Following the birth of my second son, mother was diagnosed with breast cancer. I couldn't believe those gentle mounds of mother's love could harbor a deadly disease, spreading throughout her lymph nodes and beyond. Mom had the appropriate surgery for that time, mastectomy and tons of chemotherapy. It wasn't enough.

Two years later my sister found a lump in her left breast. After a lumpectomy and scarring radiation she's cancer free. From then on, I viewed my breasts differently. Oh, they looked the same on the outside, but I was aware that one or both could morph into ticking time bombs in the future.

Well, the years have passed. My breasts no longer pass the pencil test. Last year I placed a bright yellow Ticonderoga # 2 pencil under my right breast and the damn thing stayed there! I moved from side to side, jumped a bit, but it hung in there. Droop, sag, hang, the body is losing to gravity.

The day after the mammogram Dr. Dean, my radiologist called me at school saying she needed to see me as soon as possible. My heart sunk all the way to my tummy. My principal came in to take over my third grade class and I anxiously drove to Dr. Dean's practice. An ultrasound, a CAD (computer assisted digital) mammogram, and a needle biopsy later, I found myself in Dr. Dean's private office. She said the pathology report would be ready in a few days and that she was being ultraconservative. I told her she could be as conservative as she wanted. It was my breast. I liked it and wanted it around for a long time. A week later I was in outpatient surgery at Cottage Hospital having minor breast surgery, a precaution to ward off possible cancer.

I'm fine now. If only I could get back to the small stuff, like worrying about passing "The Pencil Test."

Bobby

By Allen Zimmer

She was worried about the boy, since the divorce he seemed so angry all the time. She decided that it might help if she got him a dog.

When they got to the pound the boy was frightened by the loud barking and yelping. That's probably why he chose Bobby. The other pups were whining trying to get closer, but Bobby just sat there, his brown eyes looking quietly up at the boy. His mother said "Don't you want one of the other pups; they seem more lively."

"No," he said, "I want that one."

He thought Bobby was beautiful. He was a mix of Collie and Sheppard, with a long reddish brown coat, the same color as the boy's hair, with a white blaze on his chest, and with little black lines around his eyes, almost like mascara.

Bobby was smart. He quickly learned to sit, lie down, roll-over, and shake hands, although the boy couldn't get Bobby to shake with his right paw.

Bobby was strong. When the boy raced Bobby downhill on his Schwinn, Bobby always beat him, even when he stopped to lift his leg on a tree. Bobby was a good climber. Sometimes when he climbed over the fence, he'd be gone for a day or so, they never knew where.

One time they got a call from a man who was very angry and said his dog was in heat and we'd better keep Bobby away, or else. After that they put a picket fence on top of Bobby's fence.

Bobby was his dog, but his big sister liked to tease him by picking Bobby up and cuddle him in her lap like a baby, saying "Goochy goo." Bobby loved it, but it drove the boy wild.

He'd shout, "Stop it, he's my dog, he's not your baby, put him down." Usually she did. But this time she scooped Bobby up and began cuddling him, the boy yelled "Stop it, put him down, stop it." She wouldn't. Finally, he reached over and gave Bobby's tail a hard yank. Bobby snarled, jumped off her lap, and bit him on the arm. She laughed in triumph. Bobby crept out of the room.

The boy was furious, muttering "My dog bit me, my own dog bit me." Angrily, the boy followed Bobby into the garage. Bobby was in the far corner, lying on his back, legs apart, eyes squinting in fear. The boy grabbed a piece of rope and began hitting him, yelling "You... don't... bite... me, ...you... don't... bite... me."

That night Bobby crept up onto the bed. The boy thought, I'll show you, and pushed him down. Bobby kept trying to get up, but the boy kept pushing him down. Finally Bobby curled up next to the bed.

The next morning the boy put Bobby's food in a bowl and left for school. That was the last time he saw Bobby. At least he didn't cry that time.

Not like he did when his father left.

The Final Gift

By Sharon Alvarado

Finally   We are alone.......

I want to stretch the minutes into hours, days, months....... but there will be no miracle, no happy ever after. This will be the last time I am with you.

You lay there so familiar, yet I have never known you like this. Naked... Silent

Not a whisper of movement

For a moment my fingers rest gently at your throat, I lay my head on your chest. There is no one to see us, no one to object.

A drop of blood rests at the corner of your mouth. Your hair is damp. The blood has matted your curls. I turn your head tentatively and touch those soft tight curls that lay close to your neck. My hand moves down slowly over the muscles in your arms, your chest. I stop at your hips...... I see the tight springy curls at your pelvis. I lift and hold this... oh... so well known part of your body. Your thighs are still strong, long muscles still defined against your skin. I touch your feet and remember you standing next to me. The large smile that always greeted me, lips that brought such pleasure.

I look closely, your eyes are now closed, your mouth slack ...there will be no laughter no delight...... but I will forever remember the sound of my name on your lips.

On the table sits a basin of warm water, wash cloths and towels.

I dip the washcloth into the basin and bring it to your face. Slowly I move the cloth down to your neck, your broad shoulders....

I begin your last bath.

My final gift to you.

Missing the Deadline

By Robert A Reid

Jim was missing and the women in his life were worried.

"When was the last time you saw him?" asked the detective.

Marni thought for a minute and replied, "It was Friday, 3 days ago."

"Does he always let you know his plans and whereabouts?"

"No, after all he's my brother, not my husband, so no need to tell me his every move, but 3 days with absolutely no contact has me concerned."

The detective stroked his chin and asked. "Did he seem normal on Tuesday?"

"No he was distracted like he was under some pressure. He usually is carefree and jovial."

"Does he gamble? Use drugs? Drink to excess?"

"I don't think so, but Cheryl, his girlfriend, would know better. I called her before I called you and she hasn't seen him either."

"Okay, Mrs. Lahr I'll talk with her and keep you informed on our progress."

The detective hopped in his cruiser and made the short drive downtown to the apartment shared by Jim and Cheryl. She was an attractive young woman who invited the inspector into a sparsely but tastefully furnished living room.

"I'm so glad you're looking into this," she said, "I'm worried. We've lived together for almost 3 years and Jim has never done this before. I've texted him and left messages on his cell, but no response"

"His sister said he seemed distracted. What did you think?"

"Something was bothering him," Cheryl said, "But he wouldn't share it with me."

"Is he the type that might get so discouraged he would injure himself?"

"Oh no! --- he would never do that?"

"Any idea at all what could be troubling him?"

"Well, he's taking a writing class and complains about not finding enough time alone to sit at his computer and write."

"All right, if you can provide me with a recent picture of Jim, I will look into this. I doubt there is violence involved but his behavior is out of character and you have to wonder why."

The detective returned to the precinct and was able to get the morning newspaper to run Jim's picture the next day. About noon his telephone rang. On the line was the owner of a downtown café who said that the missing man had been eating at his lunch counter the past 3 days.

"Did he give you any idea where he might be staying?"

"No, he didn't, but there is a cut-rate flop house in our same block – perhaps he's living there."

After the short drive downtown, the detective climbed up the cluttered stairway to the dimly-lit front desk. He presented the photo of Jim to the clerk who recognized him immediately.

"He's in room 315," the clerk said. "He only goes out for meals and has received no visitors or calls."

The detective bounded up the stairs two at a time and, although he expecting no trouble, he pulled his gun from his shoulder holster before knocking.
An irritated voice came from behind the door, "Go away"

"Police, open up!"

Slowly the door opened and standing in the semi-darkness was a man who looked tortured. There were dark circles under his reddened eyes and his shoulders were sagging. In the background was the bright light of a computer monitor surrounded by several cups. The air smelled of burnt coffee.

"Are you Jim Haslund?"

"Yes----what's the problem?"

"Your sister and girlfriend are frantic with worry about you. Haven't you seen their texts and voice mails?"

"No, my phone is not on. I'm trying to write but I have a terrible case of writer's block. When this happens I just have to be alone with my thoughts and try to break the stalemate."

The detective was silent with his thoughts for a moment and then said, "Any luck?"

"No, no luck whatsoever and the class is tomorrow. I'm going to need today to try to get something on paper. This interruption has already broken my chain of thought."

Taking a moment to reflect on this zany situation, the detective advised, "Since the chain is broken, I recommend you call your girlfriend and sister immediately before you go back to work."

"Okay," Jim said dejectedly.

"And finally, I don't know much about writing or your assignment but you might consider telling the story of how you became a missing person and the subject of a police investigation trying to meet a deadline of an adult education writing class."

The Giant Anteater

By Anne Cushing Cotton

paces daintily, like a ballet dancer,
fur rippling in sun and shade;
but she walks on her knuckles, not her toes,
claws turned up and inward,
ready to rend a termite's nest
or to scratch bark from a fallen branch.

From a rubbery vacuum hose
flickers and slithers her nervous tongue
relentlessly tracking ants.
A black and white *reboso* clings
to her shoulders. Her vast and hairy tail
sweeps the dust.

My husband stands in the shadows, a quiet figure
among the noisy families.
"On the plains," he says, "the gauchos
entangle them with *bolos* and kill them."
He peers with pleasure through his new glasses.
"I don't think that happens anymore."

His gaze anticipates the anteater's tread
back and forth the length of the grassy pen,
follows her into a cave; but there is no shelter
from a mind that absorbs the endless
array of animals and objects composing the world,
assembles, tracks them down.

"There are some horrible creatures called humans," he says.
We watch the dark entrance.
Into the sunlight emerges the anteater
pursuing her quest, sniffing, licking delicately
the endless array of corners in the world
where ants and termites hide.

For John Cushing, Biologist

Saturday Morning

By Jeanne Northsinger

Noisy kids fill the theater. All week I've worried about the hero or other characters in the serial trapped in a room with mechanical walls closing in. The serial always ends with the main characters in deadly peril and the word, "Continued" with dots after it. When the next episode begins on the following Saturday, some twist saves them only to have them end up in another dire predicament like a falling elevator. We find seats, the lights go off, the thick red velvet curtain draws up and we all clap and cheer. The feature movie is usually a cowboy and cowgirl story, but first comes a cartoon and then the serial.

Entry to the Saturday morning movies requires two Model Dairy milk bottle caps. We save them up so my sister Barbara and I, and sometimes the neighbor kids, have enough to get into the movie. Early in the morning twice a week the milk is delivered to our front porch. The cream rises to the top and we pour it off into a jar to use in coffee and on cereal. In cold winter weather the milk freezes before we bring it in the house and it pushes out through the narrow necks of the glass bottles. The lids perch on top of the little frozen towers.

Saturday morning we take our bottle tops and walk to the Crest Theater, which means crossing Highway 40. We wait on the curb for the light to turn green. The trucks speeding past look like monsters, their headlight eyes set either too close together to too wide apart, their grills horrible, threatening teeth in scary grimaces.

When we reach the theater, we trade our bottle caps for a ticket with numbers for a raffle. Before the movie, a man stirs all the stubs in a large fishbowl, draws one out, and reads the numbers one at a time as we look at our tickets. One of the numbers match my ticket! As I walk up the long aisle, I hope Steven Brown is in the theater to see me. I am in love with Steven Brown. I know we are going to get married some day because once when I was changing into my swimsuit at the beach, I think he saw me. Standing on the stage I think I look cute in my blue jeans with the cuffs rolled up just so.

My prize is a beautiful little red plastic radio. I am very proud of winning that radio. It brings Art Linkletter, the Lone Ranger and Marshall Matt Dillon into our kitchen every week.

Sometimes after the movie, we go to the Spudnut Shop. For a nickel I get a glazed or chocolate donut. Once in awhile I get an apple turnover which I love. The sweet, cinnamon-spiced filling is folded inside thin, soft dough and fried. Sometimes the turnovers are still warm. But they cost a dime so I usually just get a donut.

General Sherman

By Christine Riesenfeld

Three thousand years ago, a massive tree later dubbed, "General Sherman," started life as a seed, small and light as an oat grain, weighing almost nothing. Cleopatra had not yet been born when its first green shoot emerged from the soil.

Three thousand years later, this *Sequoiadendron giganteum* or giant sequoia, as it's commonly called, stands taller than a twenty-story skyscraper and weights over twelve hundred metric tons. I can't comprehend metric measurement, but I do understand that thirty railroad cars would be needed to the move the trunk of the tree. The General Sherman tree is the largest living thing on the earth.

These massive giants live in very small neighborhoods. Sequoias inhabit only the high slopes of the western Sierra and nowhere else in the world. Their villages are getting smaller and smaller as the decades pass. The two–foot thick outer bark provides protection from wildfires. Death usually comes from an ax or bolt of lightning; the former a more effective death threat than the latter.

Unlike its even taller cousin, the coastal redwood, the giant sequoia thrives in sunlight and gathers its muscular branches near its top; allowing us a sunlit view of its fibrous, tawny-red bark. Some branches span one hundred and forty feet, farther than the height of most other trees. The mass of branches at the top beckons me to slow down, stare and bathe my body in the sunlight shared with my giant friend.

When I first approached the General, other people were staring at it and speaking in hushed tones; its looming presence stifling loud conversation and mindless chatter. Perhaps nothing needs to be said about a tree that succumbs to neither disease nor senility.

In 1875, it took two men just nine days to cut down another three-thousand-year-old giant sequoia located nearby. A cross-section was shipped to the Philadelphia Exposition for the California display. People attending the Exposition labeled the exhibit a "Californian hoax." They didn't believe any tree could grow that large.

Count me a believer.

Shadows

By Joan Jacobs

The shadow of the mountain obscures the valley.

What is taking place?

All seems peaceful.

Morning develops.

The shadow of the mountain

no longer darkens the valley.

Spring is beginning, winter receding, snow melting.

The stream runs full.

Deer and their fawns, foxes and their pups,

bears and their cubs drink the cool water.

The fish have come to the surface

after spending the winter in the stream's depths.

Fishermen ply their rods

hoping the trout will take the bait.

Farther down stream, the marshes

are filled with cattails.

An explosion of color startles the eye:

poppies, lupines, violets, buttercups,

bluebells in abundance.

Bees once again busy collecting nectar.

Apple, cherry and plum trees bud.

Birds collect what they need

to build their nests in the mighty oaks.

Meadow grass sways in the gentle breeze,

the sun shines bright,

cumulus clouds travel across the blue, blue sky.

Cows and sheep give birth to their young.

Night approaches.

The shadow of a mountain again darkens the lowland.

Time to rest.

Tomorrow, another day in the valley,

As life continues to unfold.

Revelations

"I kept waiting for the other shoe to drop."

The Plagarist

By Larry Mason

"Oh what a tangled web we weave, when first we practice to deceive."
- Sir Walter Scott

(I've often wondered if that means we simply need more practice).

After three and a half years of high school, I discovered I had met all my requirements for graduation and was free to move on to higher pursuits. But wait, I wasn't ready. I was on the varsity basketball team, and didn't even know where I wanted to go to college. So I "posted," meaning I hung around for another year, while I figured things out - and took a bunch of electives to fill the time.

My first choice was Miss Insley's Creative Writing class. I had never written anything but reports, and the idea of writing just for fun made me feel a little giddy. Imagine - writing about whatever you felt like. It was liberating to my repressed right brain, relieving it from the tyranny of its other half. I was amazed at what came out, and looked forward to each new chance to be creative. Besides, there were lots of girls in the class, unlike my other technically oriented courses. In fact, the captain of the football team and I were the only two boys - and two of the best writers (or so we thought). Ron used to joke that we would go on to become famous, which was really only half in jest. At that age, I think we actually thought we would. I did, in a way, that very semester. But it was more infamy than fame, at least in my mind.

Near the end of the semester, Miss Insley announced she wanted us to write book reports, the best of which would be submitted to a city wide book report contest. I hated book reports. Where was the creativity in just reporting what someone else had written? Besides, it meant I actually had to read a book - stuff like "Silas Marner" or "Tale of Two Cities," - assigned reading in our high school literature class. Boring. So I did the easy thing - I procrastinated. Finally, it was the day before the report was due, and I hadn't even gone to the library, let alone picked out a book.

After supper (dinner was what you ate at noon), I asked Mom if she could recommend a book - without telling her I needed to write a report for the next day.

She loved Jesse Stuart, who wrote homespun yarns about down-home mountain folk, and handed me a copy of "Foretaste of Glory," his latest success. It is a tale of people in a remote mountain town in Appalachia, and their reaction to a sudden and spectacular display of northern lights. Thinking it the harbinger of The Second Coming, they furiously try to rectify all their feuds, duplicitous relations and deceits before the dawn of Judgment Day. It was a quick and hilarious read, but sometime after midnight I found I was running out of stamina. There was no way I was going to finish the report by morning - and my own judgment day.

Then I reread the Foreword, a succinct and lyrical encapsulation of the story - perfect for a book review. It enticed the reader, explaining the thesis without revealing the plot. So I did what seemed to the only possible solution. I copied it for my book report. Of course I rephrased and rearranged, just so it wasn't verbatim - I didn't want to be guilty of plagiarism, on the outside chance that someone had actually read the book. In the morning I had second thoughts, but it was too late. The die was cast. With great trepidation, I handed it in, hoping that would be the last I heard of it. Then I prayed for absolution. But it didn't come.

Having committed what I was sure was an indictable crime of plagiarism, I prayed it would go unnoticed; or if revealed, I could just plead ignorance - or stupidity, and thus avoid a jail term or unpayable fine. What a way to start my writing career!

Ms Insley stood before us, a sheath of Book Reports in hand. "We have some *excellent reports*," she chirped, and fairly glowed as she read:

"Foretaste of Glory," By Jesse Stuart. Reviewed by Larry Mason. I slunk as low as I could in my seat. Surely someone would detect this fraud. But everyone seemed to love it and I received many admiring glances. I had to admit it sounded great:

"September 18, 1941, was no different from any other autumn day that came and went at Blakesburg....the inhabitants bent to their tasks; but when the noon whistle, courtesy of the Fire Department, sounded its shrill warning, they were more than ready to pause in the noonday heat.... All human life that ventured forth in the blaze of afternoon confined itself to the river, where the drowsy water riffled slowly over the rocks, singing a song without words, and the long arms of the

willows reached down and combed smooth water..."

Suddenly I owned this fluid prose. As far as anyone else in that room knew, I had written it. Then I remembered the biblical admonition: "To be sure, your sins will find you out." Even if they don't, they can make you feel damnably uncomfortable.

The selected reports duly read, Ms Insley announced they were to be entered forthwith in the City-wide contest. I fantasized leaving the country. How could I extract myself from this tangled web? As it turned out, I couldn't.

A week or so later, Miss Insley was positively radiant when she walked into the classroom. Had she had a proposal? Was she about to become a Mrs.? Breathlessly, she announced:

"Larry has placed second in the Book Report Contest. The award ceremony will be next Friday evening at Cathedral High School."

Was there still time to disavow it, 'fess up? But it was too late. I was doomed.

When at last the sun had journeyed beyond the backbone of the mountain, cool shadows spread across the town. The people began to stir again,

savoring the cool air from the mountain. It
would be a fine night for sleep.

But not for me. I tossed in torment. How could I
escape? Turns out, I couldn't.

In the distant north an icicle of light appeared on
the low horizon. Long tentacles of white gold
stabbed southward, slitting the velvet darkness
with lightning speed. Great splinters of light
darted across the heavens, crisscrossing each
other on rolling seas of liquid fire, as God had
promised on the last day.

Judgment Day began late, 8 pm, in the cavernous
gymnasium of Cathedral High School. All my family was
there, along with my friends, come to see me accept my
ill-begotten award. The judges had even posted our
reports in the entrance hall for all to read. The
auditorium was full. On center stage I was flanked by
two girls, who had placed first and third. Squirming in
my gray double-breasted suit, too small after three years
of wear, I had visions of Calvary - except now the thief
was in the middle. Speakers praised us, flash bulbs
popped, and sweat trickled down my armpits.

The morning broke, and with it absolution of all
sins, real or imagined, confessed or denied. The
townsfolk went about their business as if nothing

had happened. It was generally agreed that it was all an illusion, and that whatever had transpired the night before was best forgotten.

The next morning, there was my picture with the two other recipients on the front page of the Indianapolis Star. The Times and News had similar accolades in their afternoon editions. I pretended not to notice, and people were impressed by my modesty. At last it became apparent that I had gotten away with this charade. Like those of Blakesburg, the people of Indianapolis had lost interest. Still, it didn't help my internal judge. I kept waiting for the other shoe to drop, but it never did.

Until now.

Who Am I?

By Beatrix Larrick

Everyone wants to be near me. They say I warm them and make them feel welcome.

They bask in my soft light and savor my subtle scent.

Someone pokes me and no one attempts to stop him.

But then we all settle down in renewed warmth.

They linger long in this atmosphere, for they know full well I won't be here when they come again.

May I introduce myself?

I am the log that burns in the open fireplace.

A Practiced Goodbye

By Lisa Stathopoulos

Thanksgiving dawns sultry and sensuous
butter yellow amidst a wide blue bowl horizon.
She does not notice the white sands and sapphire sea
as she sips bitter coffee
to stave off the morning chill.
She does not heed the lone
pelican poised over his catch
as he glides away to deeper waters.
Lost in reverie, she can only mull
over her son's absence on this
feast of thanksgiving.

She said a reluctant goodbye to him
on those marbled steps and knew
December would reach long and hard,
tentacles squeezing her heart
yet never relinquishing her devotion and joy.
Frigid winds must blow before his return
to her unwavering adoration.
She longs to tightly hold his body,

salty, sweet to her nose,
a return to days
of childish laughter and kisses unabashed.

Now, she grasps the beauty of sunrise,
thankful for the mug's warmth.
Days of advent will fall away and bring
him close to her, yet he is already
inside, contracting her heart.
She mulls over her son's absence
knowing that on Christ's Birth,
He will once again return.

Standing Ovation

By Bob Fisher

"On your feet," Tyler hollered above the crowd's roar at Baker Field. "Get your butts down on the field. Let's go to work!"

Columbia 6, Penn 7, Half Time. October.

I hefted an unwieldy glockenspiel and trooped behind the other band members, trying to remember where I fitted into the first formation.

What was I doing in a band? I was a violinist, assistant concertmaster of the Columbia University orchestra. But I harbored a fervent yearning to be part of the glorious football spectaculars at Baker Field. It was the time of Sid Luckman and his Warriors. The time football was a Game. The time before the platoon system split football into a machine. Sid and his gang played both offense and defense the whole glorious 60 minutes.

Before the time of machine marching bands. None of us Columbia ruffians would be allowed to sort uniforms for present bands. We had fun. We had lotsa fun. The band took us into the heart of the action.

Gruff, bearded, Bandmaster Tyler Jenkins considered my request to join the marching band. With no one to play glockenspiel he set me to work on this upright xylophone. Red tassels flying, three ranks of silver bars glittering. It was resplendent in sight and sound. I made rapid progress, but soon found there was an enormous drawback. The instrument mounted square in front blocked forward sight. Why I even considered surmounting that problem- it had to be the pull of fall madness.

Practice was in a reverberating gym that mashed ears, but was nothing compared to what intricate band formations did to the rest of the body. The whistle blew. "Fisher, go left on the 4th beat. Jerry's coming in front of you and you'll bang right into him." Bang! Time and again I struggled, blinded by the huge instrument. Tyler was too soft hearted. He kept his blood pressure down even with my raging bull moves.

Then it was time. Out on the field we moved into the first formation, blatting away on some march. Thrills! Blue and gold day beaming on the Great Fall Spectacle, every throat adding to the roar cascading down on us.

Only one minor collision as we marched through all the formations. Finally a Sousa march opened the band into two wings to set up the playing for the Alma Mater. In great form I lustily banged away on the silver keys. But where were my two buddies? I glanced around the side of the glockenspiel. Oh, My God! I was alone. By myself. Totally by myself out in midfield. Panic. Almost took off running to catch one of the wings. But I stood there, alone, and played as loud as I could. The wings finally formed around me and off the field we marched. Tyler told me I had a standing ovation. Sure. Everyone stands for the Alma Mater.

Uncle Harvey Visits Le Grand

By Holly Jennings

Uncle Harvey **bumped along** in his rusty, dented Ford. Dust spewed up from the tires which were newly smeared with clay. He wheeled into the driveway, which had a better surface than the cracked asphalt leading from town. Mr. Ipsen, the Danish immigrant who had broken the clayey soil of his ranch, had grand ideas about road building. His half-mile drive winding to the house was a macadam surface lined with palm trees and oleanders that bloomed pink and white for much of the year.

Winnie watched the car jolting to a stop in the farmyard. "What's he up to this time?" she thought. She walked out and gave him a welcoming smile.

Harvey slid out of the Ford and walked to the back of the grimy car. The car was a clever ruse. A fine-tuned engine hid under the splotched paint of the hood. He untied the ropes keeping the trunk shut, pulling out two battered suitcases and a shoe shine box. Winnie grinned to see this combination. "Put me up for the night?" Harvey asked. He glanced back at

Dolly, the large French doll in the back seat as he followed Winnie around to the back of the ranch house.

"Come on in," Winnie said and opened the screen door. Harvey stepped inside, set down his cases and leaned over to remove his dirty boots. Mud flaked off the tooled leather as he set them on the shoe ledge by the door.

"I need a wash," he said and headed for the stationary tubs at the back of the porch.

"Don't be long. I'll pour you some iced tea, " Winnie replied. She took a large handkerchief from her apron pocket and wiped her sweating face. *What a day for my brother-in-law to arrive!* she thought bitterly .

They sat drinking tea at the kitchen table. "Jim out working?" Harvey asked, gesturing toward the fields.

"No, he's upstairs taking a nap."

"How's he been?"

"Not so good. That brother of yours is really down and out this time." Winnie frowned and stared into space. "Like a piece of cake? It's lemon coconut."

"Sure thing. Got a sandwich to go with it? I

haven't eaten since breakfast in L.A." Winnie made a generous meatloaf and pickle sandwich and gave Harvey a salad of sliced tomatoes and sweet, red onion. "I'll take Jim back with me. You coming too?"

"Sure thing. We can leave Dick and George to run things. What are your plans?"

"Plans. What plans?"

"Come on, Harvey! What are we to do? The boys have been running the ranch for months now. We're ready to sell out. What will we do for money until then?"

"Live offa me, I guess. No, listen here. I got me an empty place. A little cafe in Chinatown I repossessed last month. You could run it until I find a new renter."

"You know I can open the place for you, Harvey. Would that be lunch only?"

"Well, it did well at breakfast and lunch for two years. Can Jim put in a hand to help you?"

"Help with what?" Asked Jim with a scowl as he walked into the kitchen.

"We're headed for L.A. big brother. I'm in a dilemma and you are the solution."

Winnie chimed in, "Ellie and the boys can handle the chores until we get back. Harvey needs us to run his café for a few weeks."

Jim smiled his agreement.

"Now you're talking!" exclaimed Harvey. "I'll drive you two down to L.A. and we can set things up by the middle of May. I can smell the roast beef already."

Clerking Propane

By Joyce Metz

As a teenager I clerked in my father's appliance store. My brothers, Don and Dave, delivered the propane gas that supplemented the sale of stoves and refrigerators.

One day Don returned from delivering his route and was smirking broadly.

"Whatever is the matter with you?" I asked.

"Damndest thing happened today. You remember than mean dog out at the Schulz farm?"

"Sure I do. He's the nasty mutt that always barked and nipped at you. What happened?"

"Well, today that little bastard was worse than usual. I couldn't even get the hose unreeled from the tank truck and he was on me, growling and trying to chase me back into the cab. Christ, look he tore my pant leg again. I have to admit, he's a helluva watch dog, but damn, I had to get the gas delivered. No one came out of the house to rescue me so I grabbed the hose and gave that dog a blast of propane right on his rear end. God you should have seen him. He went back up the driveway like a rocket, whimpering all the way."

I laughed along with Don. "I guess you got your delivery made then."

"Hell yes that dog disappeared."

Several months later Don again delivered propane to the Schulz farm. This time no dog bothered him. Mrs. Schulz came out of the house. Don handed her the invoice and asked, "Where's the watch dog?"

"You know Don, that's the strangest thing. A couple of months ago that dog's balls fell right off. He's out there now sleeping under the shade tree, gentle as a kitten."

(For those unfamiliar with propane—it freezes on contact.)

Brian's Trick

By Lottie White

You awakened every cell of me.
It's impossible to quell the sea
of emotions that pitch, toss, heave
within my hold. I believe
you unmoored a part of me—
set depths, unplumbed, free.

For awhile, under full sail,
we skimmed the waves—left no trail
behind, we thought. Now, wary
we change direction and vary
our course. Downwind we tack—
the wind, once with us, slack.

But now I know what sailing is,
know both the dangers and the bliss.
I owe that, Brian, dear, to you—
my ever loving—loved—me too.
Yearning, longings overwhelm
my heart, while you are at its helm.

Trick—a sailing term meaning a period of time steering.

Cruisers and Crooners

By LaRae Johnson

In 1948 we left North Dakota for Richmond,
California, where Dad had been hired to teach 6th
grade. We made the move in a 1939 Plymouth 4-door
sedan. Light gray, it had a sizeable back seat; plenty of
room for my sister, Anne and me and all of our
possessions. On the three-day trip we sang songs like
You are my Sunshine (pronounced shunshine by my
four-year old sister). Dad taught us the car's license
number (5B99013) by singing it with the melody to
Jimmie Crack Corn.

When I was 16 and could drive, we had two cars.
One, parked on the street, was a 1949 Plymouth 4-door
sedan resembling a green upside-down bath tub. The
other, parked in the attached garage, was Dad's gold
1956 Chrysler Newport, his pride and joy. The narrow
driveway to the garage slanted downward at 45
degrees. Getting a car in there was a difficult
maneuver for a novice driver. So I was wiser driving
the 49er.

This car had character. Every time the steering
wheel turned the visor fell down and the radio boomed

a flatulent, loud blast. As my friends and I cruised the drag and Connie Francis sang *Where the Boys Are*, the blast would come and we laughed till we cried.

At a red light, everyone would jump out and circle the car clockwise hopping back in before the light changed. Sometimes, I would shift into first gear and rev the engine while the clutch hovered in neutral daring the adjacent car to drag race. When it screeched off we were in stitches, still at the light.

On family trips in Dad's car we passed the time playing games and crooning tunes in four-part harmonies. We even had a record player in this car, real high tech. The disc was about the same size as today's CD. If the road was bumpy, the music would skip. I don't know why Dad didn't buy more records. We only had one: The <u>Ames Brothers' Greatest Hits</u> with songs such as *You, You, You* and *Rag Mop*.

One summer we pleaded with Dad to take us on a camping trip instead of our usual North Dakota trek. But where to go? Resolution in our family was reached by playing a game of Hearts. The winner was the boss and in this case decided where we would go. The car was packed and we were in the middle of our game when the car began to back up out of the garage all by itself. So funny we all burst out laughing and laughed all the way to Mount Lassen.

One day I asked Dad for his car. I put my foot down hard on the accelerator for momentum to back up the steep driveway. I failed to notice the right rear passenger door was open. The ensuing crash shook the house and folded the car door in two. I went into the house shaking. Dad was reading the paper, his glasses hanging on the end of his nose. He didn't even look up. For several weeks I had to look at that once beautiful Chrysler with its rumpled, crumpled door taped and roped closed.

In 1961 Dad and Mom drove me to UCSB in the Chrysler. In the backseat I pondered my new life. There was no singing on this trip, but now 63 years later I'm still humming 5B99013.

The Railway Sleepers

By Brian Silsbury

On any workday, I'm dragged into consciousness by the clatter of the bedside alarm clock at around 5:00 a.m. I perform my ablutions and eat a bowl of porridge. Why such an unearthly hour? Well, I catch the 7:10 from the Petersfield station in order to get to my London office by 9:00 a.m.

As a worker-bee, I'm totally reliant on British Rail. I leave the house punctually at 6:50, march briskly to the station armed with an umbrella and a briefcase. Once I arrive, I stand in exactly the same spot on the platform. I have to be that precise so that I can be in the right place when the train eventually grinds to a squealing stop. If my judgment is good, *my* carriage is right in front of me. Why am I so particular? Because once correctly positioned, I get into the same carriage with the same people. Apart from Lex, a tall, slim, elegant professional woman, I don't even know their names and I'm only on nodding terms with the rest of the commuters.

As the train arrives, I, being fleet of foot and having sharp elbows, quickly get to my seat and settle down.

In a matter of minutes, my usual fellow commuters join me. I say usual, because we are always the same trusty travelers who sit in the same seats, back to engine or facing engine. Woe betide any 'stranger' who has the temerity to take one of our seats.

Once underway, we have the same routine. We each get out our newspapers and, depending on whether it's a broadsheet or tabloid, successfully arm wrestle, elbow to elbow, until we create the necessary space so we can read the headlines, check the financial details and do the cross-word. English reserve demands that one rarely—if—ever, speaks to his traveling companions after the initial "good morning." I always enjoy the last thirty to forty minutes when I close my eyes and take a nap. Even the beautifully coiffured Lex, nods off. Mondays to Fridays, day in and day out, this is my mind-numbing routine.

However, on Saturdays, things are different in Petersfield. With the market in full swing, the locals and commuter worker-bees mingle and exchange pleasantries. Today, it's sunny as I stroll with my son towards the high street. As we chat, I notice a vaguely familiar figure coming around the corner. To my surprise, it's my daily traveling companion, Lex. She still looks tall and almost regal, and yet she seems so different out of her smart two-piece business suit. Trotting beside her is a short, balding man. As we get closer and make eye contact, she says, "Hello Brian, this is Jim my husband. Jim this is Brian, I sleep with him every morning on the 07:10 to London!"

About the Authors...

"Old Swmr" is the license plate of **Grace Altus,** school psychologist. Her stories fill us with meets and medals, old friends wrought so skillfully we too care, and her Santa Barbara hometown tales.

Sharon Alvarado, grew up in Santa Barbara, Ca; left and returned with stories to tell. "My first writing class with Joan Fallert gave me permission to dream dreams, reveal secrets and walk in my own imagination."

At a memorial service a son said, "In all my 56 years I thought I knew my mother, but we have learned only now of her rich, full life." **Gerry Atkinson** writes so her children learn of her life before they were born, and now, after they have lives of their own.

Retired physics professor **Paul Barrett** writes about childhood experiences, attempts humor, enlivens history and sometimes sneaks in a little physics.

Betty Battey: enjoys writing class members reading their essays in the *Tales we Tell* program at Valle Verde.

Priscilla Boyan, native Vermonter, daughter of the Mayflower, one-time lab tech and college instructor, daily swimmer for 47 years

Ruby Buck was born in Brooklyn, New York in 1929. She was a long time student of Bill Downey who encouraged her interest in writing. After his death, she continued Adult Education classes with Joan Fallert. She has completed <u>Ruby's Gems</u> and is working on another book of short stories. She thanks her family and friends without whom there would be no stories to tell.

Anne Cushing Cotton is a retired French professor from University of California, Santa Barbara. She is a native of NYC, received a BA in Greek from Bryn Mawr College, her MA in English, at Columbia, was a Fulbright Scholar in Padua, Italy and was awarded a PhD in French at Colorado. Her publications include *Spring Eclogue* (1961), *Musk Ox* (1999), *Apollinaire's Alcools* (1966) and *Calligrammes* (1980) UCPress.

"I have always loved words and stories," say **Penny De Ley.** "I dabble in poetry and short story, but I think my forte is dramatic monologue—with me performing. At 71 my goal is to become a wise old woman. Not there yet."

Virginia Paxton Durbeck – Kansas born; Texas schooled; USAS wife; authored two published books, Gliding Forward, Glancing Back, and Treading the Tightrope of Time. Mantra: Don't postpone the joy of creative writing.

Paul Edwards, old Disney animator, sign painter, watercolor artist and cartoonist. Also youth minister in five different churches across the United States and WWII Navy veteran.

Bob Fisher – Start with a chemist's small grey world. Open up on wings of imagination, catalyze by Joan Fallert's encouragement. Scintillate into words, roam experiences of life. Outsize. Small. Near and far. Minor. Major. All.

Peggy Loch Hall enjoys writing childhood memories of life growing up in Santa Barbara, where both she and her mother were born. The family settled in the beautiful, but much smaller city of Santa Barbara in 1891.

Writing a story from an inanimate object's point of view is an enjoyable challenge for Chicago-born **Joan Jacobs.**

California born **Holly P. Jennings,** EST teacher, enjoys Asian travel. In her writing she tackles the peculiarities of her hometown characters.

LaRae Johnson (BA in Journalism; retired music teacher) fills her days with music, writing and art. "There's never a dull moment".

Gerson Kumin, a native of Washington, D.C., did not begin writing until after he retired. He now lives in Santa Barbara, CA where he dreams of his lost cats and remains busy with his next masterpiece for class.

Born in Logan, Ohio, **Bea Larrick** is a pet lover. Her childhood dog, a pitbull named Charles Lindberg was called "Lucky." Sight faded, Bea Larrick no longer ventures far, her pleasures simple: story read aloud, tweet of a visitor to her patio for crumbs, seed and her quiet company.

Helen Barron Liebel: author, teacher, former member California Business Education Board, Overseer Whitman College

Bill Livingstone, a retired urban planner, has taken Adult Ed's Recollecting and Writing class since 1991. He has written over 350 recollection stories, plus about 50 fiction pieces, and has been published in several magazines, including Soldier of Fortune and Reminisce, several times.

Marge Sweet Livingstone: Iowan. Probate paralegal. Newlywed.

Audrey Martinson --from United Kingdom. After WW ll moved with her American husband to Kodiak, Alaska. 23 years, 8 children, 1 mighty earthquake and tsunami later moved to California in time for the Painted Cave Fire ... disaster prone? Or just a good story?

Hoosier **Larry Mason** could never decide what he wanted to be when he grew up. Since taking up writing, Larry has discovered the magic of time travel back to his youth, where he has now decided he wants to be a writer when he grows up.

Joyce Metz admits her philosophy is, "I may grow old, but I don't have to grow up."

Three boys, second husband with five children, **Doris Wells Miller**. Playwright, watercolor artist, genealogist, bedeviled by Lupus. Enjoys life.

Jeanne Northsinger writes because writing makes it real even if it is made up. She agrees with Mark Twain and never lets the truth get in the way of the story.

Lolly Quackenbush is well known for her focus on Ducks and Lollipops. She likes to write of the bygone days.

Robert Reid is a physician who attended over 5000 births. His undergraduate degree in English Literature gave him strong interest in writing. He has written chapters in anthologies on physician—hospital collaboration, scientific papers in gynecology and continues to write a restaurant review column for the Santa Barbara County Medical Society Newsletter.

The "gift of gab" led Pennsylvania-born **Christine Riesenfeld** to the college debate team, a career in law and the lifelong love of language.

Writing is a new passion for **Marilou Shiells**. A lifelong artist, she equates writing to painting with words instead of brushes.

Brian Silsbury was born in the U.K. and moved to Santa Barbara in 1995. A management consultant, he retired in 2004 and began to write. On a whim, he sent "Memories of the Mallard" to the U.K. magazine, Evergreen. It appeared in the summer of 2008.

Lisa Christine Stanthopoulous is married to Peter and has a grown son Nicholas. She holds an MSN, FNP but left nursing to pursue writing prose and poetry. She published her first poetry book entitled Stepping Stones. She continues to write and participate in poetry, writing and literature groups.

Illinois born **Doris Thome, RN,** writes what her eyes see, ears hear, heart feels and mind absorbs – stories lived and imagined that beg to be told.

Born and raised on beaches of California and Hawaii, **Beth Thompson** came to writing after teaching elementary school for 38 years. In her second "go round," poetry, gardening, art, being with friends and grandchildren light her world.

Lottie White a native of Los Angeles lived in various locations in California before settling in Santa Barbara. A creative writer, she wrote many poems and short stories. Lottie passed away days after her 90th birthday in May 2011.

Sandra Williams entrepreneur from southern California—"writing enables me to relive experiences using creative editing as desired."

Allen Zimmer was born and raised in Southern California. He received his architectural degree from Cal Poly San Luis Obispo in 1962. After joining the Air National Guard he and his bride moved to Santa Barbara where they've raised their 3 daughters. He opened his architectural firm in 1973 and has since been responsible for many governmental, commercial and residential projects, winning 17 national and local architectural awards.